Making model

VICTORIAN STATIONARY ENGINES

Making model
VICTORIAN STATIONARY ENGINES

Stewart Hart

THE CROWOOD PRESS

First published in 2022 by
The Crowood Press Ltd
Ramsbury, Marlborough
Wiltshire SN8 2HR

enquiries@crowood.com
www.crowood.com

British Library Cataloguing-in-Publication Data
A catalogue record for this book is available from the British Library.

ISBN 978 0 7198 4120 0

Cover design by Blue Sunflower Creative

Disclaimer
Safety is of the utmost importance in every aspect of metalworking. When using tools, always
follow closely the manufacturer's recommended procedures. However, the author and pub-
lisher cannot accept responsibility for any accident or injury caused by following the advice
given in this book.

Dedication
I dedicate this book to my family.

Typeset by Simon and Sons
Printed and bound in India by Parksons Graphics

CONTENTS

1 Introduction

Trilogy of engines, left to right: vertical cross single, Grasshopper haulage engine, open frame horizontal engine.

MANY PEOPLE FROM A non-engineering background are attracted to the fascinating hobby of model engineering. These newcomers struggle at first with how to get started, and I know from experience that they can be overcome with self-doubt when they visit one of the many model engineering exhibitions and see some of the breathtaking models on display. They must put this self-doubt to one side and realize that even these expert builders were once newcomers and, like all model engineers, will have a scrap box. It is possible to build some wonderful models even with the most basic of equipment. To set up a workshop you don't need a huge amount of space; my own workshop has a floor area of just 3m2 and I know of workshops that are even smaller than this. You just need a small shed, or the corner of a garage (or if you're really lucky a small spare room) and plenty of imagination on how to best utilize the space you have.

Some of the basics you will need are a bench with a metal working vice, a small lathe, a pillar drill and a bench top grinder for sharpening tools. In addition, you will need a range of hand tools, files, hammers, etc. The assumption will be that you're familiar with the machining principles and the basics of these tools.

I am of an age and from a background where I was taught the rudiments of engineering at secondary school: schooling now, particularly in the UK, seems to bypass practical subjects with the emphasis being on more academic studies. So, before anyone embarks on setting up a workshop and taking up the model engineering hobby, I would strongly recommend enrolling in a short course that will teach them the basics. Failing this, join your local model engineering society and get involved in the club activities. If you show sufficient interest, club members will take you under their wing and adopt you as an apprentice. Read as much as you can on the subject: The Crowood Press has some excellent Metalworking Titles, and there are also some very good magazines available.

Taking the first step with a new hobby is always the most difficult. You'll find yourself inundated with well-meaning advice as to what to undertake for your first project. My advice would be to start off modestly: don't be too ambitious by jumping in and starting a 5" gauge model of the Flying Scotsman. I can guarantee that it will end up abandoned, hidden away under the bench. Start with something simple that doesn't require an expensive set of castings and look for something that can be made from low-cost bar stock material. This philosophy has influenced the designs of the three engines covered in this book.

Before you embark on building a model, it helps to have an understanding of how a steam engine works. We will start with a little of the history of stationary steam engines, a basic description of how a steam engine works and the different types of engines. The

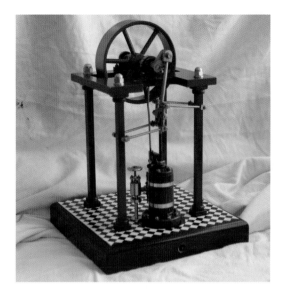

Vertical cross single.

reader will then be guided through the selection and purchase of a range of basic workshop machinery and tooling, followed by a step-by-step guide to the manufacture of three common types of steam engine.

The first engine is a very basic open frame horizontal mill engine. These types of engine were put to use in a wide range of applications. They were simple to produce and maintain and make an excellent beginner's engine and will introduce the builder to the manufacture of many of the basic engine parts.

Once some of the basic processes have been perfected, the builder will be able to move onto the

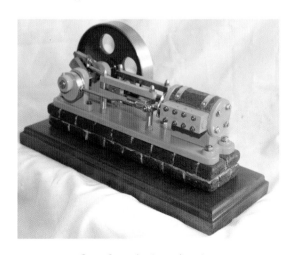

Open frame horizontal engine.

Grasshopper haulage engine.

modelling of a slightly more challenging project – a vertical cross beam winding engine – specifically of a type that was extensively used in the northeast of England coal fields. This engine will use a lot of parts common to the horizontal engine again using bar stock material.

The final engine in the series is an early example of a Grasshopper haulage engine. These engines were used extensively for hauling minerals and goods up inclines and were the forerunner of the locomotive. Again, the engine uses a lot of parts common to the first two engines but is slightly more challenging, introducing the reader to more advanced techniques. However, for those who don't want to take on the challenge of these techniques, simpler alternative designs are provided.

I designed and built these engines a number of years ago, and they were the subject of build articles in the *Model Engineer* magazine. Since their publication, I know that many examples of the engines have been built so they are well proven and practical designs, suited to the capabilities of a novice builder.

The Stationary Steam Engine

THE VICTORIAN STATIONARY STEAM engine powered the industrial revolution that changed the world. It evolved into many types and sizes of engines, providing a fascinating range of projects for the model engineer. Stationary steam engines evolved from the simple condensing engine into many different types of high-pressure engines that had a wide range of applications.

The development of the stationary engine can be traced back to the ground-breaking atmospheric engines of Thomas Newcomen's first practical fuel driven engines developed around 1712. These engines used the condensing of steam within the cylinder to create a vacuum that sucked the piston down, rocking a beam that was attached to a chain that was in turn attached to a large pump rod that activated a pump at the bottom of the mine shaft, and so drew water from a mine. These engines were gradually refined throughout the 1700s due to improvements in iron casting techniques pioneered by the Coalbrookedale Company. This allowed the manufacture of much larger cylinders, along with minor changes and refinements to the mechanics of the engines.

These early engines were very inefficient, with huge amounts of heat energy lost. This was not a problem for engines used to pump water from coal mines that had a ready supply of cheap coal. But it was a problem to the tin and copper mines in Cornwall where the coal had to be expensively shipped from the South Wales coal fields. This led to the invention of the separate condenser by James Watt that, together with further design and manufacturing improvements, increased the efficiency and the power of the engines.

Hundreds of these Newcomen and Watt improved engines had been built by the 1800s, and were employed in mines and iron works where their irregular motion was not a problem. Weaving and spinning sheds, however, required a steady, smooth motion that was being met by waterpower but as demand on

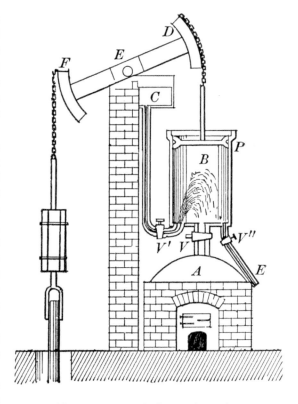

Newcomen atmospheric pumping engine.

the industry increased, sources of suitable waterpower became scarcer.

This demand for power led to further developments of the steam engine with the introduction of double-acting engines where the steam acts on both sides of the piston and the rotative flywheel, thereby smoothing out the motion of the engine. At the same time, improvements in boiler technology led to higher pressures. The Victorians called these higher steam pressures of 40-50 PSI (270-345 kPa) 'strong steam'. To the modern eye, these pressures are extremely low, but nevertheless these advances led to smaller, more powerful, less expensive and faster

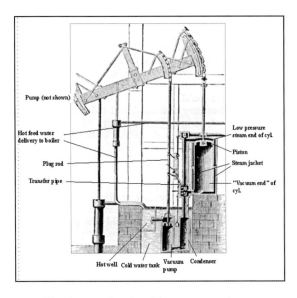

Watt improved engine with separate condenser.

Author's model of a watt parallel motion beam engine.

engines. These non-condensing engines, driven by the expansive power of steam and coupled to the Watt centrifugal governor, started to meet the power needs of the weaving and spinning sheds. Freed from the geographical constraints of waterpower, cotton towns began to spring up in and around the coal fields of Northern England, where the damp climate was particularly suitable for the spinning and weaving of cotton.

This expansion led to the development of other industries to meet the needs of these textile industries, that in turn drove a rapid expansion of other manufacturing industries. All of which needed a source of cheap, reliable power that was met by the stationary steam engine.

TYPES OF STATIONARY STEAM ENGINES

Beam Engines

The early stationary engines were a development of the Newcomen and Watt pumping engines with several subtle changes. Because they were rotative engines, it wasn't practical to connect the beam to the piston with a chain, so a fixed coupling was required. The problem here was that the end of the beam moved in an arc which had the effect of pulling the piston rod off centre, resulting in a high-wear rate

of the cylinder, piston and piston rod. This led to the invention of a number of ingenious solutions.

Watt Parallel Motion

The Watt parallel motion is based on a parallelogram – a four-sided plane where opposite sides are parallel. One of these sides is part of the beam, with one end of the opposite side connected to the piston rod and the other connected via a link to an anchor point, often the wall of the engine house. This arrangement results in a linkage that compensates for the non-linear movement of the end of the beam. Watt parallel motion found use on medium to large

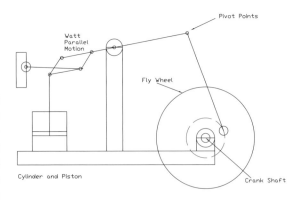

Beam engine with watt parallel motion.

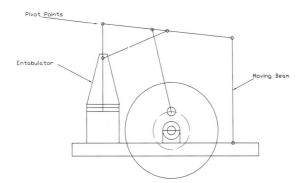

Grasshopper or half beam engine.

engines, many of which were used in the pumping role in mines, water and sewage works.

Grasshopper or Half Beam Engine

The Grasshopper engine was so called because the action of the linkage resembled the leg action of a jumping grasshopper. Another name for this type of engine is the half beam engine. In this type of engine, the connecting rod crank and flywheel is in the middle of the beam. The front of the horizontal beam is connected to the end of the connecting rod with the other end of the beam connected to a vertical rocking beam. The horizontal beam is connected at its midpoint to a link, and the other end of this link connected to an anchor point either to the wall of the engine house or to the entabulator on the end of the cylinder.

VERTICAL ENGINES

Hammer Frame Engine

The hammer frame engine is so called because the bedplate and main frame resemble a drop hammer frame. The cylinder can be mounted on the top or bottom of the frame, with the cross head operating on slides. These types of engines were extensively used as marine engines because of their compact design.

Steeple or Table Engines

The steeple engine was an early attempt for a lighter more compact engine than the beam engine.

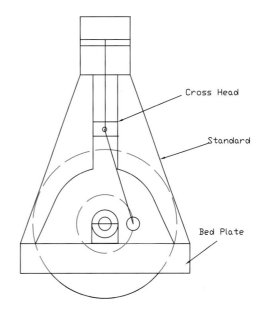

Hammer frame vertical engine.

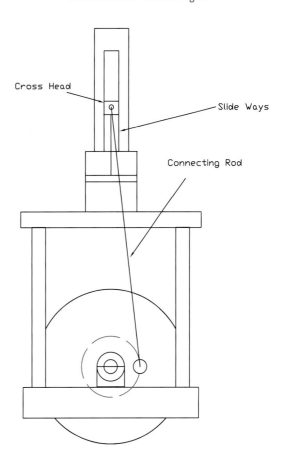

Steeple or table engine.

It consists of a cylinder mounted on top of an entabulator with slide bars mounted on top of the cylinder. Sometimes these slide bars were triangular, hence the name 'steeple' engine. The cross head working in these slide bars had connecting rods on either side driving the flywheel. It was found that these engines were too top heavy for use as marine engines, so were used on inland waterways and lakes and for powering workshops.

Vertical Cross Single

This type of engine was extensively used as a winding engine in the coal fields of the Northeast of England. The flywheel mounted on the top of the engine was also used as the winding drum. A central link is mounted on the pivot point of the piston and crank shaft, and connected at each end are two other links that are anchored to either the walls of the engine house or to supporting pillars.

HORIZONTAL ENGINES

Open Frame Horizontal Engine

The simple design of this engine resulted in thousands (both big and small) being made by a wide range of local manufactures. They were used in various applications: driving workshops, spinning and weaving mills, breweries, flint mills, etc. They could be made small enough to take on a portable roll, driving threshing machines, sawmills and fairground rides. They were truly a universal source of power. They consisted of a bedplate with a cylinder bolted

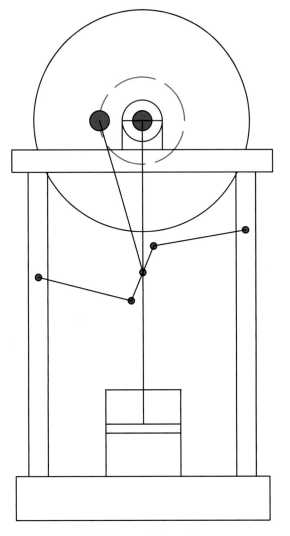

Vertical cross single engine.

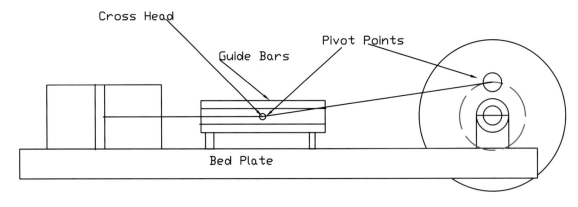

Horizontal open frame engine.

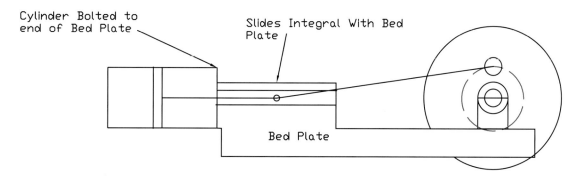

Cylinder Bolted to end of Bed Plate

Slides Integral With Bed Plate

Bed Plate

Self-contained horizontal engine.

on the top with two pairs of slide bars that the cross head worked in, that was then connected to the connecting rod that drove the crank shaft and flywheel.

Self-contained Horizontal Engine

These are like the open frame engine but were built on a more complicated cast bedplate that had the slides as an integral part of the bedplate with the cylinder bolted onto the end of the casting. This arrangement complicated the bedplate manufacture.

These are just a few of the more common types of successful engine types: but many more different types of engines were designed, some of which never got off the drawing board; others never got past the prototype stage or were financial failures. However, this doesn't mean that they aren't suitable for a model

engineering project – their eccentricity just adds to the challenge and fascination for the modeller.

COMPOUND ENGINES

With a single cylinder, 'simple' engine, high pressure steam from the boiler is fed into the cylinder that forces the piston forwards. At around a ¼ of this forwards movement, the valve shuts off to 'cut off', and

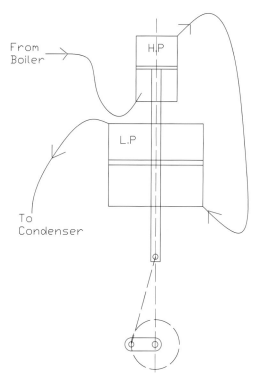

From Boiler

H.P

L.P

To Condenser

Compound engine steam flow.

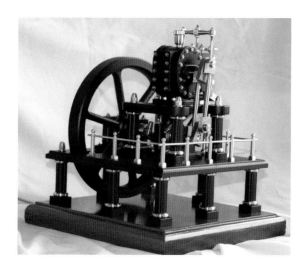

Author's model of a Simpson and Shipton engine that was a technical and financial failure.

the trapped steam expands for the remaining travel of the piston. The early cut off of the valve allows more work to be extracted from the steam. As the steam expands, its temperature reduces and with each stroke the temperature increases and decreases which is a source of inefficiency. To lessen this heating and cooling effect, the compound engine was invented by Arthur Woolf in 1804 who patented the 'Wolf high pressure compound engine'.

In a compound engine, high pressure steam enters the high-pressure cylinder from the boiler. The used steam is exhausted into a low-pressure cylinder which can exhaust into a third or even a fourth cylinder. Each cylinder uses the steam to produce power, This gradual expansion of the steam results in less heat loss. The volume of each cylinder increases to compensate for the pressure drop so each cylinder produces equal amount of work. This results in increased efficiency and power, smoother running and lighter engines with a higher power to weight ratio. These engines found great use in the marine environment.

Many early beam engines were converted to compounds by adding additional cylinders. Sometimes the cylinder was added at the same end of the beam as the existing cylinders, and on others they were added at the opposite end. These types were known as McNaught compound beam engines after the engineer who pioneered this modification.

COMMON ENGINE PARTS

For a reader not from an engineering background, a brief explanation of the names and functions of some of the main parts that are common to most stationary engines would be helpful. The names of different engine parts are not always universally used – there are some regional and industry variations, so to the uninitiated this can be baffling. Throughout the text I've kept to the same names, or I've used the names I think best describes the part so that they are obvious to the reader.

- *Bedplate:* The bedplate forms the foundation of the engine onto which other parts are attached. It is usually a large casting, but in some cases the actual floor of the engine house serves as the bedplate.
- *Cylinder:* The cylinder is the heart of the engine. Integral parts of the cylinder are steam passageway and fixing points for the valve chest, end covers and other ancillary parts.

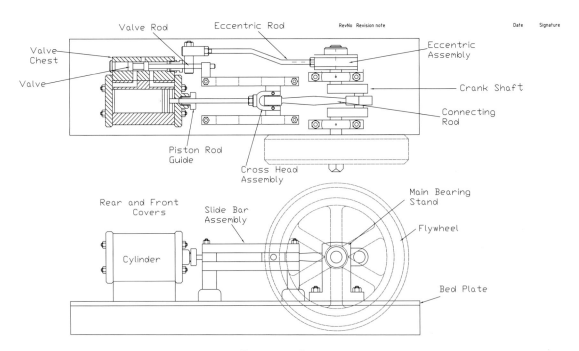

Common engine parts.

- *Piston:* The piston is fitted with a seal and is a close fit in the cylinder. Steam pressure acts on the faces of the piston moving it in the cylinder. In a single-acting cylinder, the pressure acts on just one face powering just one stroke of the engine. In a double-acting engine, the pressure acts on each face of the cylinder in turn, powering the forward and return stroke of the engine.
- *Rear and front covers:* These close and make the cylinder steam tight with the front cover, forming a stuffing box cavity to take a seal that wraps round the piston rod making it steam tight.
- *Piston rod guide:* This forms a guide for the piston rod and compresses the sealing material in the stuffing box to forming a seal around the piston rod.
- *Connection rod:* This connects the crank shaft to the end of the piston rod via a cross head assembly.
- *Cross head assembly:* This is a swiveling joint that joins the piston rod to the connecting rod. It works in a slide, or is connected to some other form of linkage, so that the piston rod moves in a straight line.
- *Slide bar assembly:* The slide bar assembly acts as a guide to the cross head ensuring that the piston rod moves in a straight line.
- *Valve chest:* The valve chest encloses the valve mechanism, bolting onto the side of the cylinder.
- *Valve:* The valve can be a slide valve, piston valve or rotary valve. It moves backwards and forwards opening or closing ports to allow the flow of steam into the cylinder or exhaust of steam out of the cylinder.

- *Valve rod:* The valve rod connects the valve to the linkage that connects to eccentric rod.
- *Eccentric rod:* This connects the valve linkage to the eccentric.
- *Eccentric assembly:* The eccentric generates the backwards and forwards motion of the valve. It consists of two parts: the eccentric itself (that has an offset hole that fastens to the crank shaft) and the eccentric sleeve that runs in a groove formed in the eccentric. The sleeve connects to the rod that operates the valve.
- *Crank shaft:* The crank shaft changes the forwards and backwards (linear) motion of the piston to rotary motion. The eccentric, flywheel and power take offs are all connected to it.
- *Bearing stand assembly:* The bearing stand bolts to the bedplate and holds the bearing in which the crank shaft runs.
- *Flywheel:* The flywheel is basically an energy store. It smooths out small deviations in the power output and so stabilizes the revolutions per minute and power output.

CYLINDER AND CRANK CONFIGURATION

There are many different ways to configure cylinders and cranks that depend on the constraints and power output duties demanded of the engine.

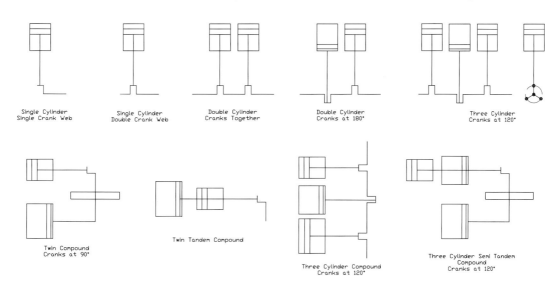

Common cylinder and crank shaft configuration.

TYPES OF VALVE

The various methods of feeding steam into the cylinder of an engine all are activated by an eccentric on the crank shaft. The three main types are as follows:

Slide Valve

Steam is fed into the valve chest and around the outside of the slide valve. The steam pressure helps to seal the face of the valve onto the face of the cylinder. This is called 'outside steam admission'. With outside steam admission, the eccentric follows the crank shaft by 90°. The eccentric moves the slide valve backwards and forwards in the valve chest. The flat face of the slide valve has a recess cut into it and the top of the valve has an adjustable connection to the valve rod. The flat face of the cylinder has three slots or ports cut into it. The two outer ports are connected via steam galleries to the front of the cylinder. The slide valve opens these ports in turn, allowing the steam to activate the piston. The middle or exhaust port is linked to one of the two outer ports via the slide valve recess allowing the steam to exhaust via the recess.

Piston Valve

This valve consists of a bobbin-shaped piston that slides in the steam chest. The steam chest has a central steam inlet and two exhaust ports at either end. The cylinder has two inlet ports and galleries similar to the those for a slide valve. When the valve is in the

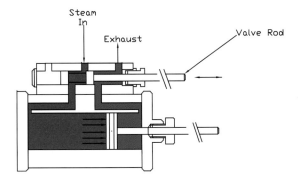

Piston Valve
Inside Admission

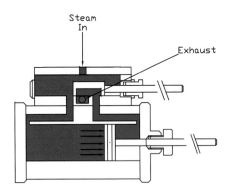

Slide Valve
Outside Admission

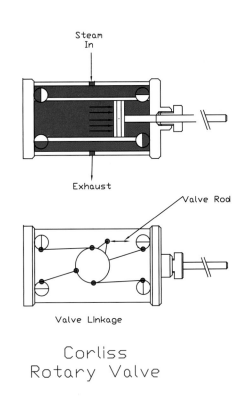

Corliss
Rotary Valve

Types of valve layout.

forwards position, steam flows through the centre of the valve feeding steam to the front of the piston. The exhaust steam flows around the outside of the valve. When the eccentric moves the valve to the rear position, steam is fed to the rear of the piston. This arrangement is called 'inside steam admission'. With inside admission, the eccentric leads the crank shaft by 90°.

Corliss Rotary Valve

The Corliss valve consist of four rotary valves – two at the top and two at the bottom of the cylinder. These are activated via links connected to a rotary wrist plate that is connected to the valve rod and is activated via the eccentric. The system incorporates trips and mechanisms that controls the timing of the opening and closing of the valves, resulting in a very thermal efficient steam engine.

VALVE GEOMETRY

So far, I've kept the explanation simple but when you get into the nitty gritty of valve geometry it becomes extremely technical, but we mustn't lose sight of the fact that we are dealing with models that are free from the constraints of efficiency, power output, speed, etc. So, I will keep things to the fundamentals, to give the reader some level of understanding.

The valve and its linkage are there to move the valve over the ports, allowing steam to enter and

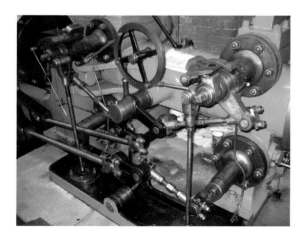
Corliss valve horizontal mill engine.

exhaust from the cylinder at the correct time with the stroke of the piston. The basic principles are the same for slide and piston valves.

Basically, the port opens just before the piston reaches the end of its stroke before it changes direction. When the valve closes it is called the cut-off point. If the cut off is 100 per cent, the steam enters the cylinder for the complete stroke of the piston. If it is 50 per cent, then steam enters for half the stroke of the piston. The reason for the early cut off is that the steam continues to expand and do useful work, meaning you're getting more work out of the steam increasing efficiency.

Lap

Lap is the amount the valve overlaps the steam port when the valve is at the midpoint of its stroke. The lap closes the steam port early and allows the steam to work expansively.

Lead

Lead is the amount the valve opens before the piston has reach the extent of its travel. It introduces steam into the cylinder before the piston has reached the end of its travel, this cushions the piston as it reaches the end of its travel, slowing it slightly before it stops and changes direction. This reduces the loading and stresses on the engine's mechanisms.

Changing Direction of Rotation

Stationary engines were put to work in many applications when they were used to power workshops via line shafting. They ran continuously in the same direction, but when they were put to use as haulage engines pulling wagons up and down inclined planes, or as winding engines in coal mines or to drive rolling mills, there was a need for them to be reversed. Depending on the valve type – slide or piston – the eccentric either follows or leads the crank by 90°, so to change the direction of rotation you need to change this relationship. The two simplest methods for reversing stationary engines are slip eccentric and Stevenson linkage. There are many other methods of reversing steam engines, but these are mostly used on steam locomotives.

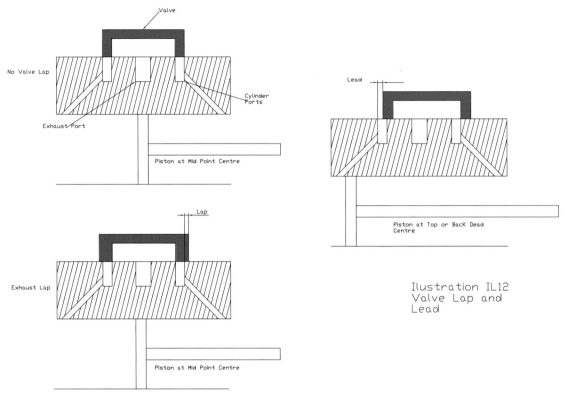

Valve layout showing lap and lead.

Slip Eccentric

The slip eccentric was one of the earliest and simplest way to reverse an engine. It consists of an eccentric that is loose on the crankshaft with stops that keep it in the correct position. To reverse, the engine is stopped and the eccentric is simply rotated onto the correct stop. There is no way to adjust the cut off with this method.

Stevenson Linkage

Despite being called the Stevenson link, it was actually invented by two of Stevenson's employees – William Howe and William Williamson (it should really be called the Willy link!). The linkage consists of two eccentrics set to work opposite each other, and two eccentric rods. The ends of these rods are attached to a slotted quadrant, with the end of the valve rod in the slot. The position of the quadrant can be adjusted by means of a linkage, when it is in the mid (neutral) position there is no movement to the valve. When the quadrant is moved to either end, the rod and eccentric at that end become active and operate the valve. Moving the quadrant to the other end makes that end active and the engine reverses. This system not only reverses the

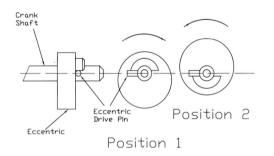

Rotating the eccentric from Position 1 to 2 Changes the direction of rotation

Slip eccentric.

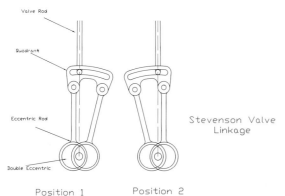

Stevenson valve linkage.

Author's model of a micro scale vertical marine engine with Stevenson linkage.

engine but also allows small incremental adjustments of the valves allowing longer or shorter valve opening. Cutting off the steam admission earlier in the stroke allows the steam to work expansively in the cylinder by using the steam more efficiently. It allowed an engine to be started under load at long cut off, and once momentum had built up to shorten the cut off.

CONTROLLING THE SPEED OF THE ENGINE

There are a number of factors that affect the speed of an engine: steam pressure, engine loading, valve setting, and the general wear and tear condition of the

engine. The simplest speed control is a steam valve operated by the Mk1 human being. This is fine for some applications, such as a mine haulage engine. But in other applications, like driving a workshop or textile mill via line shafting, it becomes important that a constant speed range is maintained.

FLYBALL GOVERNOR

The flyball governor or centrifugal governor was invented by the Dutch mathematician, physicist and inventor Christian Huygens in the early 1700s to control the speed of windmills. The device consists of a

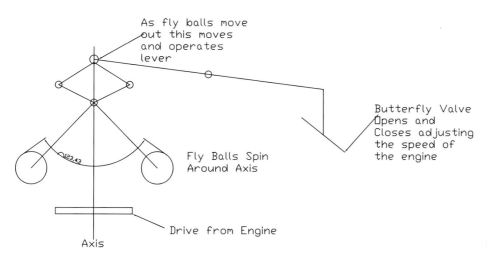

Flyball governor.

number of balls driven by the engine that are connected to a steam valve. As the engine speeds up, the balls move out due to centrifugal force, causing the valve to close due to the linkage as the engine slows the balls fall and the valve opens: this is a feedback loop. James Watt took up this idea and developed his first in 1788 subsequently giving his name to this type of governor that became widely adapted. Centrifugal governors, that are far more sophisticated, are still in wide use today.

LINE SHAFTING

A stationary engine is only part of the solution for powering a factory containing many machines. Without the use of line shafting, stationary engines would never have powered the industrial revolution. Line shafting was in use way before the invention of the steam engine. It was probably first used in wind- or water-powered corn mills. Line shafting is basically a means of transmitting power from its primary source via a rotating shaft throughout a workshop. This primary source of power could take the form of wind, water, animal, steam or electrical.

Flyball governor for controlling an engine's speed.

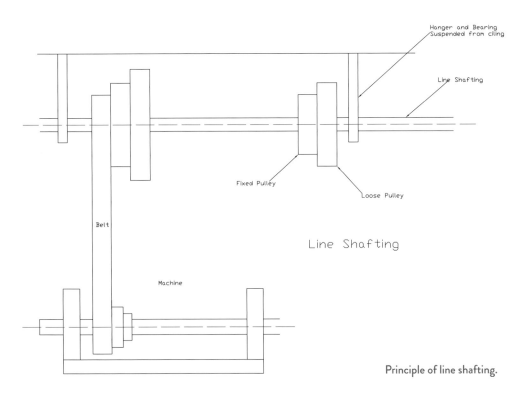

Line Shafting

Principle of line shafting.

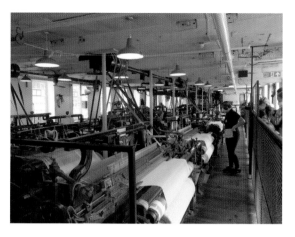

Line shafting powered weaving shed at Style Mill, Cheshire.

Line shaft running in a bearing hanger.

The power would be taken from the primary source by pulleys and belts that would drive a shaft suspended from the ceiling or wall running the length of the workshop. This system of belts and pulleys is known as the 'millwork'.

One pulley at the end of the parent shaft would receive the power from the power source. Spaced out along this shaft would be other pulleys which would be connected to the workshop machinery. By varying the size of the drive pulley, a range of different machinery could be run at different speeds. An idler pulley that runs free on the drive shaft was also used. Machinery could be stopped by transferring the drive belt over to the idler pulley, so stopping the machine without the need of stopping the primary power.

In its earliest form, the shafts were wooden. These were eventually superseded by steel shafts that were about 2" in diameter and made up of lengths that were bolted together via flanges. It was important that these shafts were carefully aligned to avoid excess stresses and wear, or even the risk of breaking the shaft. The shaft ran in phosphor bronze bearings situated in the hangers and required regular oiling and maintenance.

The earliest form of transmitting power between the pulleys was via rope belts running in grooves around the pulley. These later gave way to flat belts on a flat pulley. These belts were made of leather or cotton duck impregnated with rubber. The pulley was initially made of wood, but in time this gave way to iron or steel.

The line shafting system was very successful and resulted in some factories in the late 1900s having over a mile of shafting spread over a number of floors. With the advent of electrification, many of the prime movers were replaced with large electric motors. In time, line shafting was gradually replaced with more efficient individual small motors driving single machines. However, some line shafting was still in use in the 1960s.

Line shafting is of interest to some model engineers as it makes a wonderful project to produce model dioramas featuring a stationary engine powering a workshop driven via line shafting. I've seen some fascinating and wonderful dioramas at exhibitions featuring model workshops driven via line shafting.

3 A Basic Workshop

BASIC EQUIPMENT REQUIRED

What is meant by 'a modestly equipped workshop'? This is the basic equipment I assume such a workshop would have:

- Lathe of about 4 ½" swing
- Pillar drill of about 16mm capacity
- Drill vice
- Bench vice
- A selection of files
- Other hand tools hammers, etc.
- A set of drills metric or number drills plus a few other drills
- Some measuring equipment – a digital calliper, 0-25 micrometre steel rule
- Marking out tools, scriber, odd leg callipers, centre punch, etc.
- Some taps and dies
- Tail stop centre
- Dial test indicator

There is no provision for milling, not even a vertical slide for the lathe, and no soldering equipment. The assumption can also be made that the workshop owner would have limited experience and knowledge.

Just a couple of points about the kit required: there has been a lot said about the merits of second-hand western machinery or buying new Far Eastern-produced machinery. Whatever route you take you must be prepared to carry out some work on your machinery to bring it up to scratch. My own lathe and mill were produced in the Far East; they were cheap, and unfortunately it shows. The manufacturer's quality control has a lot to be desired. I had to strip the machines down in order to install them into my workshop. It was at this point that the faults began to reveal themselves. They were mainly about poor workmanship on assembly: casting sand not cleaned away, screws loose or the wrong size, some broken parts. I was able to correct these faults with support from the UK suppliers, and in fact some suppliers have comprehensive 'how to guides' on their websites.

These problems are not unusual as many of my model engineering friends have had similar problems. In some instances, a complete machine required replacing. The importers of these machines accept these problems as an everyday occurrence and never seem to quibble about correcting the problem.

With western machinery, when new, the build quality would have been first class, but second-hand machines would more than likely have had a hard life, with parts being worn, broken or lost by the time they end up on the second-hand market. Undoubtedly there are some very good second-hand machines out there, but the hard part is finding them. So, it pays to view the machine and see it working, and to take someone along with you who has some knowledge of machinery. It's up to you which route you take, but at the end of the day you have to learn how to get the best you can out of what you've got. Just think about the wonderful work our grandparents produced with very basic machinery.

PILLAR DRILLING

Drilling machines are one of those bits of kit that people tend to take liberties with regarding safety. In fact, if used wrongly it can be a very dangerous. People have a tendency to hold onto parts whilst drilling, but all it takes is for the drill to snag when it's breaking through for it to snatch the work out of your hand and to spin round and slash into your hand. I had a work colleague lose the tip of his thumb that way. Properly clamped work not only improves your own safety, it will also improve the quality of your work, so you will need some clamping devices. A simple G-clamp is very convenient to use or a T-nut and bolt with a bar and packing is as good as anything.

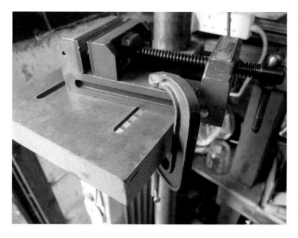

G-clamp being used to safely secure a drill vice.

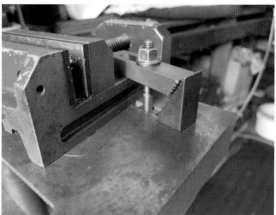

T-nut and clamp used to safely secure a drill vice; note use of riser block.

T-nut and clamp and riser block.

When it comes to the drill vice, try and get the best vice you can afford. You will struggle to produce decent work with some of the budget vices as they are not very robust, and their sliding jaws have just too much slack in them. A half-decent vice is an investment you won't regret. Also consider fitting a stop to it; you will find it will make things easier and improve the quality of your work. Likewise, you will find investing in a set of parallels will be money well spent.

An accurate method of locating and starting the drill off in the right place is required, the method used will be dependent on the degree of accuracy required. At its simplest, a good deep centre pop will stop the drill wandering offline, but this centre pop needs to be in the correct location. There are optical centre pop positioning aids on the market that can improve accuracy. A centre drill in conjunction with a centre pop can also be used. For improved positional accuracy you will have to resort to the good old sticky pin method. This is a simple dressmaker's pin stuck to the chuck with plasticine, or Blu Tack. With the drill running at low speed, simply nudge the point of the pin with a piece of wood or a screwdriver handle until it is running true. With the aid of a magnifying glass, you can now use the point of the pin to accurately locate the part. Start with a centre or spotting drill

The drill vice is an important purchase as it can greatly affect the quality and ease of your work. There are a lot of cheap, budget vices available that will cause you considerable problems due to their design and quality of construction. It is well worth splashing out on a good quality vice that will serve you well for many years.

Points to look for in a good quality vice:

- A useful size of vice is one with a jaw width of 3" to 4"
- A close-fitting moving jaw. A small amount of play in the jaw is acceptable because it allows the jaw to move smoothly in the body, but a jaw that is too slack will tilt the work out of square. Its base, sliding face and top need to be parallel to each other, and its sides and fixed jaw needs to be square to its base. This is because these vice features will affect how a part is gripped, what you're doing in effect is transferring the accuracy of your vice into your work.
- A 'V' cut horizontally in one of the jaws allows round bars to be gripped flat. You sometimes also get a vertical 'V' cut in jaws of some larger vices.

I prefer vices that don't have slotted wings to allow clamping. My preference is for a flat-sided vice as this allows the vice to be used on its side, adding to its usefulness.

It's best not to buy off the internet, but rather visit a supplier where you can handle the goods; a model engineering show is a good place to buy. Look for the general fit and finish of the vice. If it looks rough, pass it by. Take it out of the box and see what the play in the moving jaw is like. Try two or three examples and choose the best. It pays to be fussy.

There may be instances where the small amount of tilt in the moving jaw detracts from the class of work you're trying to achieve by pushing the work out of square. This can easily be corrected: all you have to do is to grip a round piece of bar at roughly the midpoint between the moving jaw and the work. This has the effect of clamping the work hard up against the square face of the fixed jaw by bypassing the tilting effect of the moving jaw.

Work needs to be gripped parallel to the base. There are several ways of doing this. Parallels come in sets – they are basically a pair of bars that have been ground to the same thickness and come in a range of thicknesses. To use, you simply sit a pair in the vice and put the work on top, tighten vice onto the work, tap the work to sit it down on the parallels, any machining you then do will be square and parallel to the vice.

A good vice is shown on the left; not so good on the right.

Sets of parallels; at least one good set is advised.

With a good quality vice, another way of gripping a part level in the vice is to place the part on a flat surface. The bed of the drill will do nicely for this. With the vice jaws open, place it on top of the part and simply close the jaws onto the part so that it is being held level with the top of the jaws.

The addition of a stop will also greatly improve your work quality and productivity. There are various types of stops available on the market, but they are easy enough to make. I fixed mine to the vice by simply drilling and tapping a hole into the vice body. A modification like this won't do the vice any harm.

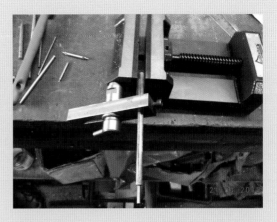

Homemade vice stop.

Parallels in use to ensure work is held flat.

Vice – extending its use by using it on its side.

Using a sticky pin to accurately position a part for drilling.

A range of drills.

then follow up with the drill – this way the drill won't wander off position. This is the best method for accurately locating the 3mm diameter inlet and 4mm diameter exhaust ports in the engines valve chest.

When buying drills again, beware: many of the budget sets on the market are not really up to the job. Buy from one of the well-known model engineering suppliers. A high-speed boxed sets of drills, sized 1mm to 6mm in 0.1mm steps, is all you need to make this engine, plus a few larger sizes for roughing out the cylinder, etc.

Centre Drill and Spotting Drills

Basically, these do similar jobs. They cut a cone to give a start and a lead to the drill proper. They come in a range of sizes so choose a size that's appropriate for the hole you are going to drill. The bigger the hole, the bigger the centre/spotting drill you want. Don't be too stingy about how deep you go – the deeper the better. You can't really go too deep and the worst that can happen is the hole will have a nice, neat chamfer which is something you can take advantage of. Centre drills have a small pilot diameter giving a lead for a 60-degree cone. Spotting drills don't have this pilot and are ground to cut from its centre. They also come in a range of sizes with 45- or 60-degree points. When I was a lad, I can't recollect coming across spotting drills. Centre drills seemed to have been universally used, but spotting drills only seem to have come into their own with the

advent of CNC machining – probably because they are less prone to break.

Cross Drilling

There are a number of different ways to accurately drill across the centre of a round bar. One favoured way is to use a drill bush – its diameter and hole is the same as the part. You simply grip this with the part in the vice and use it to locate and guide the drill on centre. Another little trick is to trap a ruler with a point on the radius of the bar, move the vice until the ruler is sitting level using the Mk1 eyeball and when it's on the centre of the bar clamp the vice down centre drill and drill to size.

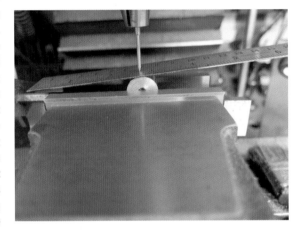

Using a ruler and a pointer to centre a round bar for drilling – off-centre tilt.

Different ways of starting a drill, left to right: centre pop, spotting drill, centre drill.

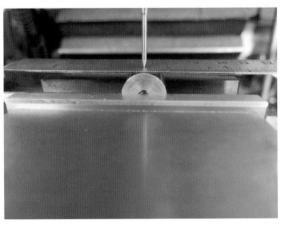

On centre level by the Mk 1 eyeball.

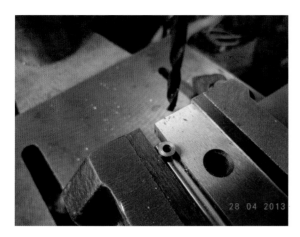

Using a bush the same diameter as the bar to cross drill.

Lathe Work

The lathe is often described as the queen of the workshop and was probably one of the first ever machine tools invented. Even the most basic lathe is a very adaptable tool, and capable of carrying out a wide range of machining processes other than simply turning a diameter. There are many publications dealing with this, so it's a subject well worth exploring just to get yourself familiar with the basics.

Lathe Chuck

There are three main types of lathe chucks. A self-centring three-jaw chuck is the main chuck used for gripping round components. It comes with two different types of jaws that extend the capacity of the

chuck. We will have some examples of this when we come to build the engines.

You can get two types of four-jaw chucks: self-centring and independent. With the self-centring, the jaws move in unison in the same way as with a three-jaw and is used to hold square bar. With the independent four-jaw, each jaw moves independently of the others (it does what it says on the tin!). You can take advantage of this for holding the engine's cylinder to machine the flat to take the valve chest. You can also use it for positioning an off-centre hole, as for the eccentric, or the 6mm through-hole in the steam chest. The simplest way to locate the part is to first mark out the part and to centre pop or centre drill the location required, and then to use a wobble

A range of 4" diameter chucks, from the front clockwise: self-centring three jaw, independent four jaw, self-centring four jaw.

Selection of chuck jaws, left to right: soft jaws, reverse jaws for larger diameters, standard jaws.

Example of versatility of an independent four jaw chuck.

Independent four jaw with wobble bar and dial test indicator being used accurately position a part.

Face plate being used to machine a 5" gauge loco wheel.

bar located in the pop mark and supported by the tail stop at the other end. Then, with a dial test indicator on the bar, move the chuck jaws so that the bar is clocking zero.

The independent four-jaw is the most useful of the chucks. I've got all three types of chuck in 5" size, but when it came to purchasing a larger chuck I just obtained an 8" independent four-jaw that I've found extremely useful and adaptable.

Lathe Face Plates

These are basically a flat disc attached to the lathe spindle. The disc has slots and holes for clamps to attach awkward shaped components to the plate for

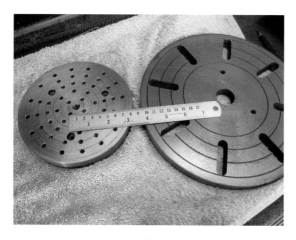

A range of face plates.

machining. Face plates are useful for machining large flywheels.

Lathe Tools

People often make the mistake of thinking that tools with tungsten-tip inserts are the best thing since sliced bread – they couldn't be more wrong. These tipped inserts are primarily produced for industry where time is money, and a high rate of material removal is the name of the game; this isn't so in a home workshop. Apart from the high cost of the holder and inserts, they are designed for industrial machines that are far more powerful and solidly built than a small home workshop machine. They are designed to knock the material off: just watch a few machining videos to see what I mean. If you want to use tungsten tools there is nothing wrong with a set of brazed tungsten tools; they are relatively cheap and work very well if kept sharp. To sharpen tungsten, you will need a green grit silicone carbide wheel. These are relatively soft wheels, and create a lot of dust, and are not much use for anything else, and tie up one end of your grinder. My preferred way to sharpen tungsten tools is to use a diamond lap, and this needn't be anything complicated. You can purchase a cheap 2" diameter diamond cut off wheel and simply mount it on a backing disc using a Dremel type arbour grip it in the lathe and sharpen the tool by hand. Or, if you like, you can power the disc using a 24V 775 electric motor mounted on a homemade grinding rest.

High-speed steel tools are readily available in various sizes of square or round tool blanks that can be

A range of tungsten-tipped tools, left: inserts right: brazed.

Diamond wheel mounted for use.

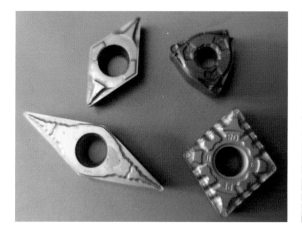

Tipped tungsten inserts tools the lumps and bumps are to break up the chips.

Homemade diamond lap.

Diamond cut off wheels.

easily ground up into a wide range of tool shapes. Many textbooks have lists of angles and rakes for various materials, but don't get too hung up on this. The main thing is to grind them up with positive rakes sloping away from the cutting edge. If a tool doesn't cut well, they are cheap enough to grind back and start again. Whilst writing this it reminded me of a story my father had about a work colleague who was a bit of a rough and ready sort of guy, a true man of the soil, but a very experienced and excellent practical machinist. At a job interview, he was asked about tool geometry. His answer was legendary: 'If you put a clog nail in, it will cut.' This is basically correct – it will cut but only for a short time and with a very rough finish.

Cutting oil does three main things: lubricates the tool, cools the tool and flushes away swarf chips. In

Range of cutting oils.

an industrial environment, cutting oil is very important as it increases the rate of metal removal, improves surface finish and cuts down machine time. It can be neat cutting oil, or it can be water-soluble, and it is fed to the cutting tool via a pump. But putting its use in the context of a home workshop, one of its big disadvantages is that the stuff gets everywhere. It leaks out of the machine tray and sprays around, covering the workshop and soaking clothing. The modeller will end up stinking of the stuff – a sure way to anger senior management. In actual practice, I very rarely use cutting oil – everything is cut dry. On the rare occasions I do use it (when cutting particularly tough steel or cutting a thread with a tap or die) I apply it neat with an oil can. The only other time I use a cutting oil is when taking a finishing cut on aluminium where a squirt of WD40 will improve the finish.

TRICKS OF THE TRADE

All crafts have little tricks, and metal trades are no different. An apprentice to any vocational trade picks up tricks as a natural part of his training by watching and learning from his apprentice master. The apprentice often won't realise that he has just picked up a trick – it will just be something that is the right thing to do. A lot of the trade skills are learnt subliminally. I once read a book called *The Wheelwright's Shop* which was basically about making wooden farm carts. Apprentices to the trade were only taken on at the early age of thirteen or fourteen so that their young bodies would develop the muscles to be able to work

with the hand tools. The bit of advice I would have for any novice is the same advice my father always gave me: always try and do your best. Remember that not everything will work out at the first time of trying; things will go wrong but the important thing is to try and learn from your mistakes and have another go, and then another and another. Persistence will eventually lead to success.

ORGANIZE AND PLAN

Try and organize things so that you make parts from the same type of material at the same time, cleaning down and saving the swarf in a builder's bucket for re-sale to the scrapyard. A bucket full of brass/copper swarf is worth about £20. (Remember the three Rs: reduce, re-use, recycle.) I usually end up owing the scrappy £20 by finding even more useful bits of scrap material while I'm there. Look for opportunities for making parts using the same type of set up, such as doing all the four-jaw work at the same time or making more than one part from the same length of bar such as for the covers. All these little wrinkles improve your productivity and, strangely enough, the quality of your work as well.

KEEPING THINGS SQUARE

Keeping features square is another critical process that you need to master. This is mainly controlled by the accuracy of the machine and the set up used. Pay

Tail stop die holders.

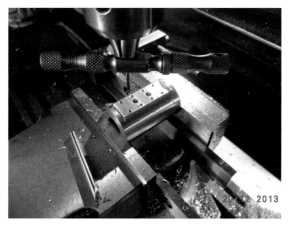

Using the pillar drill to tap square.

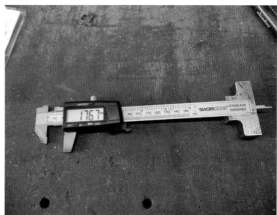

Digital calipers modified for marking odd legs.

Tapping stand.

Method of griping work level with the top of the vice.

particular attention to cutting threads square. Threads are cut square in a lathe by using tap or die holders that are held in the tail stop. I made my own holders; it's a nice little tool-making project that results in a useful bit of kit that will greatly improve the quality of your work. If you fancy taking on the project but don't like the idea of turning the Morse taper, things can be simplified by using a plain bar gripped in the drill chuck to guide the holder. As a last resort, blank Morse taper holders can be bought from many of the suppliers to the hobbyist.

MARKING OUT

Accurately marking out a part for subsequent machining is a critical operation that will affect the functioning of the finished part. So, you may consider making yourself a set of odd leg digital callipers. All you need is a cheap digital calliper and to cut the legs back with a small Dremel cut off disc (the legs are glass hard), thus bringing marking out into the digital age.

HOLDING SMALL PARTS

All too often, people make the mistake of cutting just the right length of bar to make a part only to find that there is no way for them to hold it to work on (I've got that T shirt). If you do as much work on the part as you can whilst it is on the bar, many holding problems solve themselves.

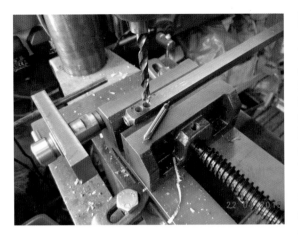

Keeping small parts on the bar until nearly completed solves griping problems.

FITTING STUDS

The design makes extensive use of stud fixings to secure most of the major parts. One problem though in using studs is getting all the studs to protrude at the same length, making things look untidy. The solution to this problem is quite simple once you know how. All you have to do is makes the studs 1mm or 2mm longer than required. Assemble the parts together, but put two or three extra washers under the nuts, then all you have to do is file the studs down level with the nuts, remove the extra washers, reassemble replacing any nuts you damage when filing, and you end up with a nice neat assembly with all the studs protruding the same length.

FILING BUTTONS

Filing buttons are used as a guide to neatly file a radius onto components. They are often held in place whilst the radius is filed with a screw or a bolt, or even a clamp. A lot of people make filing buttons from silver steel that they harden. I like to make them out of mild steel as a disposable item. A mild steel button won't damage your file by taking the sharp edge off if you should catch it. In most applications you are only using one area of the button, so if it becomes worn you can turn it round to an unused area so you can use it on multiple parts. Once worn out, chuck it away and make another. You can often engineer a button to help you hold a part whilst you file.

USE OF ADHESIVES

The designs make extensive use of adhesives. I use Loctite adhesive for no other reason than brand loyalty from my working days. There are other equally good suppliers that you may use. In describing the grade, I've merely described what it does: high strength, bearing fit, thread lock, etc., so just choose the grade that best fits that description. There's definitely a knack to using adhesive. I used to tease a work friend by saying that he learnt to glue at nursery school; this was my way of saying that he used more adhesive than was required. Only the adhesive in the joint is contributing to the strength – the rest is just a waste.

Filing button with radiused part.

WORKSHOP SAFETY

My old dad always said that a good way to test if someone was a good machinist was to count their fingers. He was of a generation where health and safety was often an afterthought, but I think there was an element of wisdom in his black humour. What he was saying was you had to be careful when you were using machinery, and this holds good today.

Anyone can have an accident, all it takes is just a moment of carelessness – you are rushing, you are distracted, you are tired, you are ignorant of the danger. All these things and more can contribute to a dangerous incident. Mostly you are lucky, and you have a near miss but the more near misses you have, the closer you are to that life changing accident. So, if you've had a number of near misses, stop, take stock of your situation and try and think what you are doing wrong, and change your methods and working behaviour. Simple things like always wearing a pair of safety glasses, don't have loose clothing (ties are

One of my own near misses Dremel burr embed in roof when it flew out of the chuck.

a no-no around machinery), don't stand in the direct line of revolving parts, and don't let your grandkids loose in your workshop unsupervised.

I was fortunate to have served an engineering apprenticeship that was extensively based on vocational training. That consisted of twelve months in an apprentice training shop where you were taught the basics followed by three years' workshop experience under the tutelage of a skilled apprentice master along with college day release and night school. This training taught us the correct and safe methods and procedures to carry out a task. Being young, you didn't always appreciate or listen to what you were told, but the apprentice masters had a way of dealing with this in that they all had a repertoire of blood-curdling stories that were sure to get your attention.

I always remember a master who went by the name of Duffy who had lost two fingers under a slotting machine whilst he stood talking with his hand resting on the machine. If he thought you weren't paying attention, he'd hold up his mangled hand and say, 'Watch what you're doing, lad, or you'll end up ordering four pints and only getting two!'

So, safety is an important aspect of any metalworking activity. Tools and machinery are potentially dangerous and should be used in strict accordance with the manufacturer's recommendations and current health and safety regulations.

CHOICE OF UNITS AND MATERIALS

The drawings are all in metric and I have used metric screw threads, as they are the industrial standard in Europe. Metric screws and thread-making tools are easily obtained and relatively cheap, though for those who are metrically challenged other thread systems may be used. The taps and dies required are shown in Table 1, and Table 2 shows a list of Imperial and Unified equivalents. Many of the parts for each engine are identical or very similar to each other, however, regardless of their similarity, all parts for each engine have a unique identity number and a letter prefix: H for horizontal engine parts, V for vertical engine parts and G for Grasshopper parts. Where parts are identical or very similar, I will only describe their manufacture once to avoid repetition.

I've chosen materials that are not costly and are easy to obtain so scrapping a part won't be a financial disaster. Wherever possible I've avoided the use of costly copper-based alloys; most parts are made from mild steel or aluminium. I have only resorted to a copper-based alloy for bearings and other small parts, but don't get too blinkered regarding material choice – use any suitable material you have. Even though the drawings are metric, the bill of material also calls up the nearest imperial size. This is because

TABLE 1: THREADING TOOLS REQUIRED

SIZE	TAPS	DIES
M 2	2nd and plug	Yes
M2.5	2nd and plug	Yes
M3	2nd and plug	Yes
M4	No	Yes
M5	No	Yes

TABLE 2: METRIC: BA: UNIFIED THREAD EQUIVALENTS

METRIC	BA	UN COURSE	UN FINE
M2	9	1-64	1-72
M2.5	7	3-34	3-56
M3	6	4-40	4-48
M4	3	8-32	8-36
M6	0	¼-20	¼-28

ENGINE FEATURES – THEIR FUNCTION, CRITICALITY AND DESIGN CONSTRAINTS

Try and understand how the engine works and recognize what the important features are. Don't be misled into thinking that getting a part to the exact size on the drawing is the most important thing. For a one-off model, it's not. What is important is getting the correct fit and alignment between parts. Size only becomes important if you are like Mr Ford and Mr Volkswagen, and are making hundreds and thousands of interchangeable parts that must fit correctly to any one of a thousand mating parts. In that case, accuracy and tolerance are paramount. Let's consider the cylinder and piston in our engine; what's important is that you have a nice sliding fit of the piston in the cylinder. Bore the cylinder first, concentrating on getting it parallel with a nice smooth finish. It is then a relatively simple task to make the piston a nice sliding fit in the bore.

Constraints on the engine design

Everything made or designed by man will have been influenced by constraints of some form or other, be they financial, technological, infrastructure, etc. The modestly equipped workshop and the assumption of an inexperienced builder being the dominant constraints on the designs of these engines. Therefore, the engines have been designed around standard material bar stock sizes, and with a valve system that avoided the need for milling and soldering, and where simple basic machining processes are required. Therefore, the models are designed around a simple piston valve arrangement that complies with these constraints.

I always try to gather inspiration for an engine design from an actual working engine even though my final design may only be loosely based on the actual engine. It acts as a useful starting point and base line for its proportion. It's never my intention to produce an exact scale model of the original; my design constraints exclude this objective. What I'm aiming for is a model that has a passing resemblance to the original, but must be a working model.

many of the suppliers to the hobby still supply to the old imperial standard sizes.

PLANNING

As with any project, it pays to take some time to study the design and to plan how you are going to make it. One of the most important aspects of this planning stage is to decide on the sequence you're going to make the parts. Look how parts fit together and decide what parts you need to make first, so that you can use them as jigs to spot through onto mating parts so that they fit together correctly. Avoid the temptation to make the bedplate first; many beginners make this mistake and wonder why the thing won't fit when they come to the final assembly. The bedplate should be one of the last things to make, and you make it to fit the parts that you have.

4 Open Frame Horizontal Mill Engine Component Manufacture

WHEN **I** FIRST SAW the engine at the Northern Mill Engine Society at Bolton, it was hidden away in a corner smoothly ticking over amongst the giant engines of the collection. It is the smallest engine in the collection. This lovely little horizontal engine is believed to have been built by S. S. Stott Ltd of Haslingden for special use as a portable engine for taking from site to site to be used as a source of power when carrying out engineering work. This was before the days of widespread electric

power. When the cylinders of large engines became worn, it was common practice to re-bore the cylinders on site. This small engine would have provided the power for the re-boring equipment which was clamped to the cylinder that was being re-bored.

The engine has a lovely simplicity about it: the more I studied it the more I began to realize that this engine could form the basis of a simple beginner's project. I have made no attempt to accurately scale the engine. I simply took lots of pictures and

Horizontal engine built by S.S.Stott Ltd, exhibited at the Northern Mill Engine Society, Bolton.

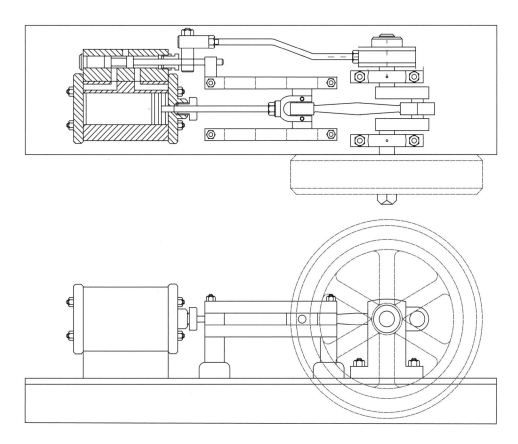

Part H1:- General Assembly

H1 plan and side assembly drawing of horizontal mill sheet 1 of 7.

used these as a means of keeping things roughly in proportion. I have taken liberties with the design to meet the constraints of simplified manufacture, but at the same time I have tried to retain features that will have a passing resemblance to the original.

The model has a 16mm bore with a 32mm stroke. It sits on a bedplate 220mm long by 55mm wide and uses a 4" diameter flywheel that can be fabricated or, if wished, a cast 4" Stuart flywheel may be used. In order to keep the material costs down as far as possible, expensive copper-based alloys have been avoided.

TABLE 3: BILL OF MATERIALS FOR HORIZONTAL MILL ENGINE

The Bill of materials for the engine is for those of you who are tempted to build this engine so you can start gathering the materials together. Most of the materials are standard imperial sizes as I struggled to find a supplier to the model engineering community who stocked standard metric sizes. For each part, I've stated the minimum length required to make that part to aid a scrap box rummage. If you study the list, you will see that you may be able to combine the material for some parts. For example, the cylinder cover material can also be used for the cylinder by turning it down to size, but that's something you will have to work out gradually in order to get the best out of your resources. If you're planning to build all three engines, 12" lengths of material will make them all. Don't get too hung up about the choice of material; in general you can use what you have available. The only thing you should avoid is running aluminium on aluminium as this tends to pick up on itself and seize.

TABLE 3: BILL OF MATERIAL FOR: HORIZONTAL MILL ENGINE

PART NUMBER	DESCRIPTION	QUANTITY	MATERIAL	SIZE
H2	Cylinder assembly	1		
H3	Cylinder	1	aluminium	32mm dia* 50mm 1 1/4" dia*2"
H4	Valve chest	1	aluminium	16mm square*50mm 5/8" square*2"
H5	Front cover	1	aluminium	35mm dia* 50mm 1 3/8" dia * 2"
H6	Rear cover	1		
H7	Piston rod guide	1	brass or aluminium	10mm h * 25mm 3/8" hex * 1"
H8	Valve rod guide	1	brass or aluminium	18mm dia * 25mm ¾" dia * 1"
H9	Valve guide stuffing box	1	brass or aluminium	10mm dia* 25mm ½" dia* 1"
H10	Piston valve	1	stainless steel or silver steel	6mm dia* 25mm ¼" dia* 1"
H11	Air supply connector	1	brass or aluminium	22mm dia*25mm 7/8" dia* 1"
H12	Valve chest end closure	1	brass or aluminium	10mm dia*25mm
H30	Base	1	aluminium	16mm square*50mm 5/8" square*2"
H13	Piston and cross head assembly	1		
H16	Cross head	1	mild steel	½"*3/8"* 2"
H18	Cross head pin	1	mild steel or silver steel	¼" dia* 2"
H17	Slide bar	2	mild steel or brass	¼" square 2"
H19	Thrust washer	2	brass	12mm dia* 25mm ½" * 1"
H14	Piston rod	1	stainless steel or silver steel	4mm dia* 75mm
H15	Piston	1	brass or stainless steel	20mm dia* 25mm ¾"*1"
H20	Connecting rod assembly	1		
H21	Connecting rod	1	mild steel	¼"* ¾"*3"
H22	Little end bearing	1	brass or phosphor bronze	10mm dia* 25mm 3/8"*1"
H24	Bearing brasses	2	brass	¼" squ * 2"

PART NUMBER	DESCRIPTION	QUANTITY	MATERIAL	SIZE
H23	Bearing end cap	1	mild steel	¼"*1/8"* 1"
H25	Cross head slide bar assembly	1		
H26	Slide bars	4	mild steel or brass	¼" squ 12"
H29	Slide bar spacer and valve rod guide	1	brass or mild steel	¼"squ *1"
H27	Slide bar spacer	3	mild steel or brass	¼"squ *1"
H28	Slide bar pillar	4	mild steel or brass or aluminium	20mm dia* 100mm 5/8" dia* 4" or hex bar may be used
H31	Valve rod and eccentric assembly	1		
H32	Valve rod	1	silver steel or stainless steel	3mm dia*55mm 1/8" dia*21/4"
H33	Eccentric rod	1	silver steel or stainless steel	3mm dia*90mm 1/8" dia*4"
H37	Eccentric sheath	1	mild steel or brass or aluminium	32mm dia*25mm 11/4" dia*1"
H36	Eccentric assembly	1		
H38	Eccentric inner	1	mild steel or brass	32mm dia*25mm 11/4" dia *1"
H39	Eccentric outer	1	mild steel or brass	32mm dia *25mm 11/4" dia *1"
H34	Valve rod coupling	1	mild steel	6mm dia *30mm ¼" dia *11/8"
H35	Eccentric rod coupling	1	mild steel	6mm dia *30mm ¼" dia *11/8"
H40	Crank shaft assembly	1		
H41	Crank pin	1	silver steel	6mm dia *25mm ¼" dia *1"
H42	Crank shaft	1	silver steel	8mm dia *120mm 3/8" dia *4 3/4"
H43	Crank webs	2	mild steel	¼"*1/2"*3"
H44	Bearing stand	2	mild steel	5/16"*1 ½"*4"
H45	Main bearing	2	bass or phosphor bronze	3/8" dia*1"
H46	Fabricated flywheel	1		
H49	Rim	1	mild steel welded tube	100mm dia*4mm wall* 25mm

(continued)

PART NUMBER	DESCRIPTION	QUANTITY	MATERIAL	SIZE
H52	Spoke plate	1	mild steel	100mm square * ¼" thick or 100mm dia
H51	Hub	1	mild steel	1" dia*1"
H48	Hub washer	1	mild steel	1" dia*1"
H50	Crank shaft spacer	1	mild steel	½"*1"
H47				
H53	Base plate	1	aluminium MDF or chipboard	¼"*2 ¼"*9" 25mm thick MDF

COMMONALITY OF PARTS

As this book covers the manufacture of three engines that are based around several common parts, this first engine will cover these common parts. When I get to the second and third engines, I will only describe the parts and techniques specific to that engine.

One last thing before we start and begin to cut metal: these small engines don't produce a lot of power. If things are too tight it won't work, so when it comes to fits it's best to work on the slack side; as my old dad used to say, 'A little bit of clearance never got in the way, son.'

PART H2 CYLINDER ASSEMBLY

As I have pointed out, the sequence that parts are made in is important and it pays to take some time to study the drawings and work out the best sequence. So, a part can be used to mark up the hole positions of its mating part, so parts assemble correctly together.

PART H4 VALVE CHEST

We make this part first. It is made from 5/8" square aluminium bar cut from a good 50mm length, allowing plenty for cleaning up. Roughly set it up in the independent four-jaw and face it off. You don't need to bother getting it running true at this stage. Then, on the cleaned-up face mark out the position for the valve bore and accurately put in a small centre pop mark.

To set it up true in the independent four-jaw, you will need a wobble bar. You can make one of these yourself from a bit of silver steel about 10mm diameter. Clocking it up true and centre drilling one end, flip it round in the chuck, clock it true again and turn a 60-degree cone on the end. If you have a solid centre with a female centre in the end this could also be used.

Wrap a bit of drinks can around the square bar so you don't scar it with the chuck. With the point of the wobble bar in the centre pop mark and the other end supported by a centre, rotate the chuck by hand and clock the wobble bar true. With the part now accurately positioned in the chuck, put in a nice deep centre followed by a 5.9mm drill. If you have one, follow this up with a 6mm reamer. If not, just try the fit of the 6mm bar that you will make the piston valve from. As drills have a tendency to cut oversize, you may find you have a good fit already. If not, put a letter A or a 15/64" drill down and try again. If that doesn't work, stick a 6mm drill down: what you are after is a nice sliding fit. Finish off by opening out with a 7mm drill for the 5mm deep counter bore. Flip the bar round in the chuck and face it off to length.

Now we need to accurately mark out the position of the two 3mm diameter inlet ports and the two 4mm diameter exhaust ports and the 1*4mm diameter inlet. Don't centre pop them as this will lead to inaccuracy. What you need now is the famous sticky pin; this is just an ordinary dress making pin held on the drill chuck with some plasticine or blue tack. With the drill in slow speed, just gently nudge the point of

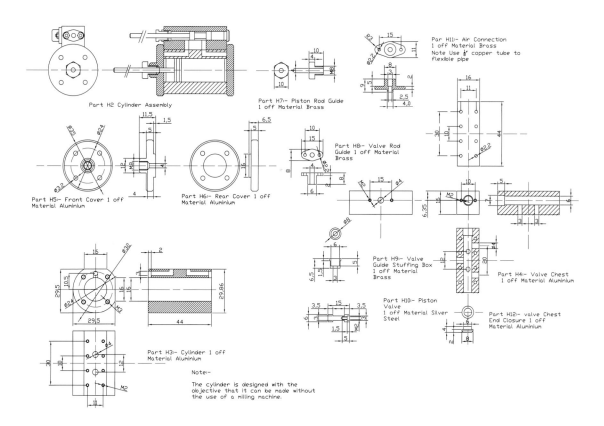

Sheet 2 of 7 basic cylinder and valve chest.

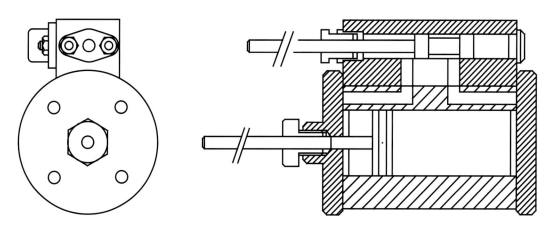

Part H2 cylinder assembly.

the pin with a piece of wood or the plastic handle of a screwdriver until it's running true. Now use the pin to accurately position on the cross lines, clamp the vice securely to the drill table, centre drill and then drill 3mm through into the 6mm bore. Don't unclamp the vice from the table. For the second hole, you need to centre up the sticky pin again, slack the vice jaws and slide the part along the jaws until the cross

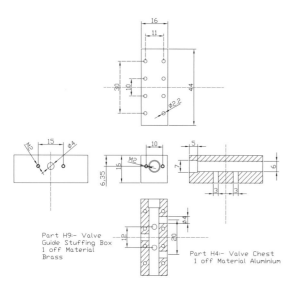

Part H4 valve chest.

Accurately setting up valve position using centre punch mark, wobble bar and Dial Test Indicator.

Position for valve bore accurately marked and centre punched.

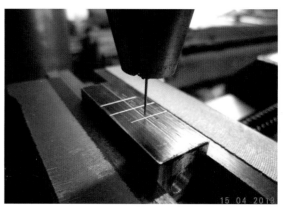

Accurately setting up position for drilling ports using sticky pin method.

lines line up. Then centre drill and drill 3mm. Repeat this procedure for the 4mm exhaust holes and the single inlet hole – that's the most accurate bit of drilling done.

Mark out the position of the eight 2.2mm diameter clamp down holes. The accuracy of these is not so important, so you can centre pop them. To position them on the drill you can use a centre drill – just line the point of the drill up on one of the marks. Clamp the vice to the drill table, centre drill and drill though with a 2.2 drill or a number 44 drill for a M2 clearance hole. Make sure the parallel is positioned so that the drill misses it. Keep the vice clamped to the table, slacken the jaws and slide the part along to the next position. Drill the hole, then the same for the

Accurately drilling ports: note vice clamped to table and use of parallels.

Drilling clamping holes for steam chest: note use of centre drill.

Marking out covers: note use of magnetic digital protractor gauge.

next and the next. When you've got one side done, turn it around to do the next side – they will all be the same position from the edge. The two M2 holes for the valve rod guide are still required, but we will drill these when the guide is made, so put the part away safely.

FRONT COVER PART H5 AND REAR COVER PART H6

These are made from a bit of 13/8" diameter bar. Skim up the diameter and face off. Black the face with a marker pen, put in a tiny centre mark so that you can use it to scribe the 24mm pitch circle diameter (PCD) with a set of compasses. Then, with a scriber set on centre, scribe a line across the bar. Zero up a digital protractor on one of the chuck jaws, rotate the chuck so that it reads 90 degrees (they are magnetic so will

stay put) and scribe a second line across the bar. You can do a similar trick with a spirit level.

Keeping the part in the chuck, remove the chuck from the lathe, centre pop the hole positions, locate the drill on a pop mark using a centre drill, clamp the chuck to the drill table and, if you wish, you may also clamp a couple of bars up against the chuck to act as stops. I had a big V block so used this centre drill. Then drill 3.2 or 1/8" for M3 clearance deep enough to make both covers, rotate the chuck against the stops to locate the next position and repeat until all four holes are drilled. You don't need to use the stops, but it does help to keep thing consistent.

Return the chuck to the lathe. Using a parting tool, face down to form the 16mm diameter register for the rear cover. Carefully measure this up and set the cross-slide dials to zero. For the front cover you are going to form the boss on what is the back of the bar so you can turn and tap for the piston rod guide, so

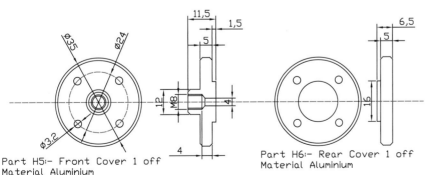

Part H5:- Front Cover 1 off
Material Aluminium

Part H6:- Rear Cover 1 off
Material Aluminium

Part H5 and H6 front and rear covers.

Drilling front and back covers in tandem. The bar is retained on the chuck.

Completed covers.

move the parting tool along and wind it in until you reach the zero. You can now part the rear cover off. Turn the 12mm diameter drill through 4mm for the piston rod, and drill and tap M8 and part it off from the bar. Doing it this way will keep everything concentric. If you wish, you can gently grip on the rear cover register and carefully machine some fancy bullseye rings in the face.

Cylinder Part H2

This is made from 32mm or 11/4″ diameter aluminium. In my material stash, I had some 31.5mm diameter bar that's near enough to the right size. As there was nothing to take off the diameter, I simply cut a 50mm length off, gripped it in the three-jaw, and faced it off. I then put in a deep centre drill and followed this up with a series of drills, finishing off with

Turning covers in tandem using part of tool to form diameters.

Parting off front cover after tapping.

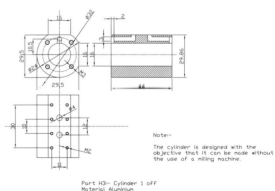

Part H3 cylinder.

a 15mm diameter drill – the nearest drill I had to the finished size. I then used a homemade boring bar to finish the bore off to size, using the bosses on the covers as a gauge to judge size. The boring bar is a simple, no-nonsense affair. It is just a piece of ½ bar with a 6mm cross hole to take a piece of broken centre drill, ground up as a boring tool held in place with a cap screw. A few pointers when boring: I like to sneak up on the final size by gradually reducing the depth of cut – this way you reduce the spring in the bar. When you reach the final size, zero the dials and put this cut through a number of times to take the spring out of the bar so you get a nice parallel bore. Don't forget to back the cut off before winding the bar back, or you will end up with a nasty spiral groove down the bore. With aluminium, a squirt of WD40 does wonders for

Cylinder mounted in independent four-jaw for facing flat.

Homemade boring bar.

Using set square to set cylinder square for facing second flat.

Cylinder bored out. Note range of drills used to rough out for boring.

the finish. Flip the piece round in the chuck and face off to length.

Put the independent four-jaw in the lathe and, with the cylinder protected with some drinks-can shim, mount the cylinder crosswise in the chuck. Make sure it's sitting hard up against the chuck face, and face off to give a 15mm wide flat. Set it back up in the chuck, but this time use a set square to set the flat face at 90, and face off another 15mm wide flat.

Black up one of the faces and mark the position for the inlets. These don't need to be drilled as accurately as the holes in the steam chest, but you have to be careful that you don't break through into the cylinder. If your drilling machine has a depth stop, you can set this up or you can make a simple collar to fix to the drill to act as a stop. Repeat on the other face,

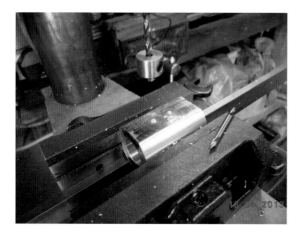

Using drill stop to fix drilling depth.

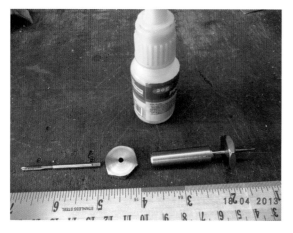

Temporary mod to tap to assist tapping.

the tap by hand, stick a bush to the tap with super glue. I used some hex bar for this, but plain bar is just as good. Then, all you have to do is grip the sleeve in the drill chuck so that it keeps the tap square and start turning the tap by hand to get it started nice and square. To retrieve your tap from the sleeve, you can break the glue's hold with a little heat (150°C).

Mark the end of the cylinder with the position for the 3mm air way and centre pop. Stand it upright in the vice set up on the centre pop, centre drill and drill down 3mm until you meet up with the 4mm hole. Then do the same to the other end. With a square section Swiss file, connect the hole up to the bore of the cylinder with a small groove; you'd be surprised at the number of builders who had failed to do this and wondered why the engine wouldn't run. Position one of the end covers on the cylinder, check

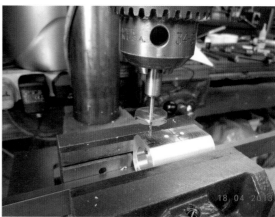

Tapping square using guide.

but this time drill and tap M3 for the bedplate fixing screws.

Clamp the valve chest onto the cylinder and, using the same size drill as you used to drill the chest, spot through to mark the cylinder. Drill M2 tapping drill size 4mm deep – you can use a stop if you wish for this as well. If you don't start the tap in square when you assemble the studs, they won't stand square. This is compounded when the mating part has to slide over 8 studs. If they are all leaning this way and that way, it becomes next to impossible to fit the part without resorting to opening the holes up or using a needle file on the holes to make it fit. If you have a tapping stand, all to the good, but if you don't you can press your drilling machine into doing the job. All you need to do is to make a sleeve that is a nice slide fit on the plain diameter of the tap. Then, so you can turn

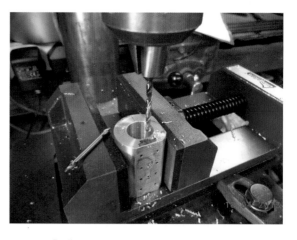

Drilling air way down the side of the bore.

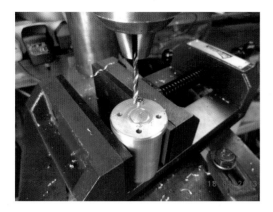

Spotting through rear cover in the correct orientation.

Completed cylinder. Note passage from bore to air way.

that its orientation is correct and spot through one hole position. Remove the cover and drill and tap this hole. M3 replace the cover in the same orientation, this time holding it in place with a cap screw, and spot through for the other holes. Remove the cover and drill and tap M3, not forgetting to mark the cover and cylinder with a small centre pop so you can put them back in the same orientation as they were drilled. Repeat with the cover for the other end, but this time mark each part with two centre pops so you don't end up assembling them back to front and wondering why they don't fit.

Cylinder Base Part H30

This is made from the same 5/8" square aluminium bar that is used for the valve chest. Simply cut a piece off allowing 3-4mm for finishing, face it to final length

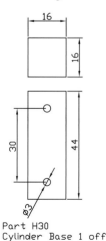

Part H30
Cylinder Base 1 off
Material Aluminium

Part H3 cylinder base.

in the four-jaw and drill the 3.2mm or 1/8" diameter for M3 clearance.

Piston Rod Guide Part H7

I made this from brass 3/8" hexagon bar, but it could be just as effectively made from 3/8" diameter bar. It's a simple enough job – just turn down the step and thread M8, centre drill then drill through first 3.5mm then follow up with a 4mm finishing drill and part off.

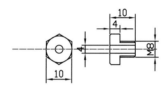

Part H7:- Piston Rod Guide
1 off Material Brass

Part H7 piston rod guide.

Valve Guide Stuffing Box Part H9

Another simple job: just turn the 8mm diameter and drill through 3mm, part off gripping it back in the chuck, drill 6mm diameter to depth.

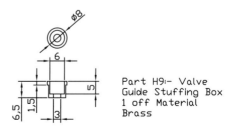

Part H9:- Valve Guide Stuffing Box
1 off Material Brass

Part H9 valve guide stuffing box.

Valve Rod Guide Part H8

Turn the 6mm diameter to a nice slide fit in the stuffing box. Centre and drill through 3mm diameter and part off, then scribe across the centre. On the scribed centre line at 10mm centres, drill two 2.2 diameter holes. With the aid of two M2 nuts and cap screws and washers, carefully file the lozenge shape to the guide. It's now time to finish off the valve chest, assemble the stuffing box and valve guide. Spot through the guide to locate the two M2 holes, drill and tap M2.

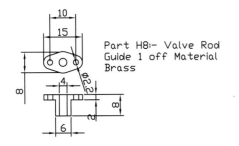

Part H8:- Valve Rod Guide 1 off Material Brass

Part H8 valve rod guide.

Spotting through onto steam chest.

Filing valve guide to shape.

Air connection Part H11

The air connection is similar to the valve rod guide. The short 4mm diameter fits into the 4mm diameter air inlet on the valve chest to help give an airtight seal. I soft solder a short length of 1/8" copper tube onto it. I connect it to the compressor using the clear flexible tubing that is used for car windscreen washers; you can get lots of this stuff from car scrap yards.

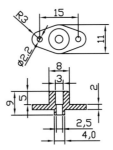

Par H11:- Air Connection 1 off Material Brass Note Use ⅛' copper tube flexible pipe

Part H11 air connection.

Piston Valve Part H10

I made this from 6mm diameter stainless steel, but it could be just as well be made from ¼" diameter bar and it could be silver steel (drill rod). It is one part where care is required, so try and work as close to the drawing sizes as you can as they are important features for the correct functioning of the valve. Start by using a parting tool to machine the 3mm diameter by 8mm wide gap. Leave about 1mm on the ends for finishing, and part off. Chuck back up and carefully face one end off so you bring the 6mm diameter at that end to 3.5mm wide. Swap it round in the chuck and do the same for the other end. As a sanity check, the part should now be as-near-to-damn-it 15mm long.

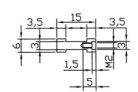

Part H10:- Piston Valve 1 off Material Silver Steel

Part H10 piston valve.

Machining piston valve.

Complete piston valve parts.

Facing off to size and drilling and tapping.

Centre drill and tap M2. Don't forget to drill the 3mm diameter by 1.5 deep counter bore: this is an important feature as it acts as a register for the valve stem and pulls everything concentric.

Valve Rod Part H32

This is made from 3mm diameter silver steel. Put the bar in the lathe chuck, clock it true and turn down to length and thread M2 using a die. The backs of dies

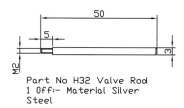

Part H32 valve rod.

don't have the same lead in as the front: the front is the side with the lettering on. So that you thread as far up to the shoulder as possible, turn the die round and run it down again, I left the valve rod over-long at this stage.

Piston Rod Part H14

This is another part that I made from stainless steel, but silver steel would be just as good. It is made in a

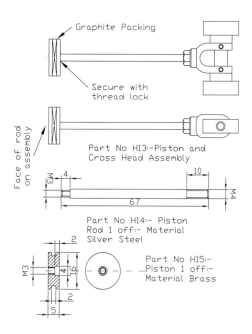

Part H13 piston and cross head assembly.
Part H14 piston rod.
Part H15 piston.

similar manner to the valve rod except it is threaded at both ends.

Piston Part H15

I made this from a bit of ¾" brass hexagon bar that I picked up at the local scrap yard. I prefer to stock up on hexagon bar as it is more useful than round bar, and it's easy to change a hexagon into a round but not so easy to change a round into a hexagon. You pay by the weight so it doesn't cost you any more: –

phosphor bronze or even stainless steel may also be used. This can be made in one operation; just simply turn down for a nice running fit in the cylinder. I've found the best way to do this is to use the actual cylinder as a gauge. First aim for a slightly tighter fit, then put in the groove for the piston packing, then using fine grade emery cloth polish to achieve the running fit. Drill and tap M3 again not forgetting the 4mm counter bore, and part off.

Connecting Rod Assembly Part H20

Parting off piston. Note groove for packing.

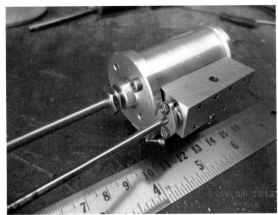

Completed cylinder assembly.

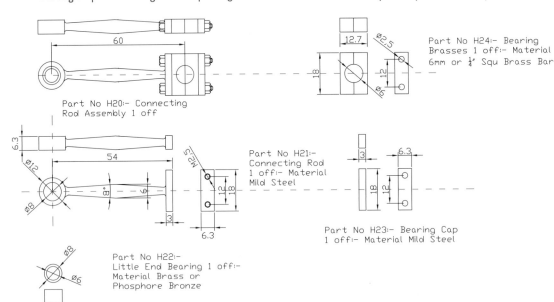

Drawings: part H20 connecting rod assembly; part H21; connecting rod; part H22 little end bearing; part H23 bearing cap; part H24 bearing brasses.

Connecting Rod Part H21

This is made from a ¼" x 3/4" x 70mm long bit of mild steel, and it is made by turning between centres. Start by marking the centre of the bar along its length and across its ends. Also mark the centre of its width across the ends, and mark and centre pop the location of the 8mm hole.

One quick and simple way of gripping a part level in the vice is to first put the part on a level surface, then put the vice over the top of it and tighten the jaws onto the part. Turn it over and the part is nice and level with the top of the vice jaws. Locate on the centre pop for the 8mm hole, clamp the vice to the table centre and drill through 8mm. Set the part on end in the vice and on the centre line and put in a centre drill. Do this at both ends.

Making dead centre.

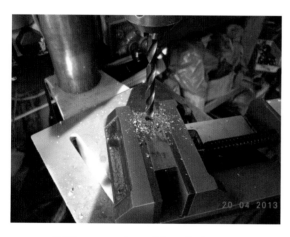

Drilling connecting rod 8mm for bearing.

Turning between centres. Note dead centre set back in chuck; the work is being driven by the side of the jaws; the front supported by small homemade running centre.

Centre drilling for between centres turning.

Completed connecting rod end finished off using filling buttons.

SMALL RUNNING CENTRE

One problem you may come across when using a running centre is that they are quite large, making it difficult to get the tool post close to the work especially when turning small diameters. The only way to get round this is to extend the tool out from the tool post, but this results in the tool being poorly supported. What's required is a smaller running centre, but a search of the various suppliers came up blank or what was on offer was painfully expensive, I then came across a small live centre for use on 'CO Baby Lathes'. All that was needed was to adapt a M3 blank morse taper arbour to take one of the CO size live centre.

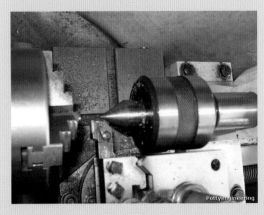

Large clumsy running centre restricting small diameter work.

M3 blank morse taper and a small CO running centre.

The taper in the head stock of my lathe is M3, the same as my tail stop, so it was a relatively straightforward to turn down blank morse taper down perfectly concentric to match the diameter of the centre. As the harbour is heat treated, its outer layer is relatively tough, so I found that this is best done with a tungsten-tipped tool aided with some cutting oil. As you get the diameter down, the material gets softer and the machining easier. With the diameter turned down, face off then centre drill and rough drill, and then bore to achieve a nice push fit on the CO centre. All that remains is to secure the centre in place with high-strength Loctite.

Turing up M3 blank in lathe head stock.

Boring out to take CO running centre.

CO centre secured with Loctite to make a much smaller running centre.

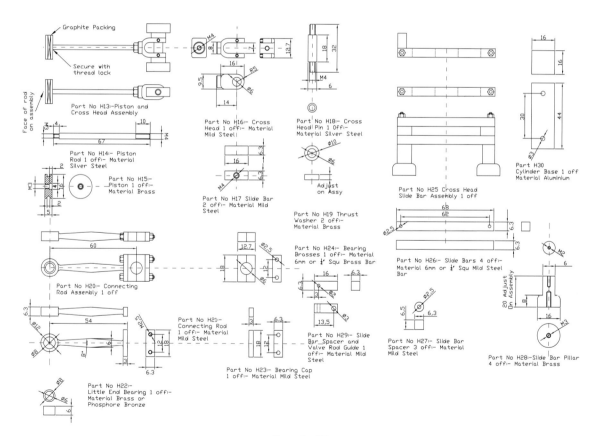

Graphite Packing

Secure with thread lock

Face of rod on assembly

Part No H13:- Piston and Cross Head Assembly

Part No H14:- Piston Rod 1 off:- Material Silver Steel

Part No H15:- Piston 1 off:- Material Brass

Part No H16:- Cross Head 1 off:- Material Mild Steel

Part No H17 Slide Bar 2 off:- Material Mild Steel

Part No H18:- Cross Head Pin 1 off:- Material Silver Steel

Adjust on Assy

Part No H19 Thrust Washer 2 off:- Material Brass

Part No H20:- Connecting Rod Assembly 1 off

Part No H21:- Connecting Rod 1 off:- Material Mild Steel

Part No H22:- Little End Bearing 1 off:- Material Brass or Phosphore Bronze

Part No H23:- Bearing Cap 1 off:- Material Mild Steel

Part No H24:- Bearing Brasses 1 off:- Material 6mm or ¼" Squ Brass Bar

Part No H29:- Slide Bar Spacer and Valve Rod Guide 1 off:- Material Mild Steel

Part No H25 Cross Head Slide Bar Assembly 1 off

Part No H26:- Slide Bars 4 off:- Material 6mm or ¼" Squ Mild Steel Bar

Part No H27:- Slide Bar Spacer 3 off:- Material Mild Steel

Part H30 Cylinder Base 1 off Material Aluminium

Part No H28:- Slide Bar Pillar 4 off:- Material Brass

Sheet 3 of 7.

To turn between centres, you can use a catch plate with a drive dog, but I chose to use my four-jaw self-centring chuck as the drive dog with a dead centre. To make the dead centre, a piece of scrap bar was first turned up with a 60-degree cone on the end; this was then set back into the chuck and the part slotted in the gap between the jaws onto the dead centre. The other end was supported with a running centre. The part was first roughed out using a parting tool and a pip turned at the little end. Then, using a radius tool, the compound slide was slewed over 3 degrees and the taper turned towards the big end. The part was then flipped around and the taper turned towards the little end. Finally, the big end was faced off to 3mm wide. If you use a ½ centre, you can go across the full width but that is something I don't have, so I left a pip, but this was easily cut off and filed flush.

Using a filing button, file the eye on the little end and drill and tap the big end 2xM2.5 for the studding that will hold the bearing brasses in place.

Little End Bearing Part H22

This is made from brass and is a simple part to make. Simply make it a tight fit in the connecting rod and secure with bearing fit Loctite.

Bearing Brasses Part H24

It always puzzles me why they are called brasses; I guess it's just one of those expressions that gained popular use in Victorian times. These are made, as chance would have it, from 1/4" square brass. Start

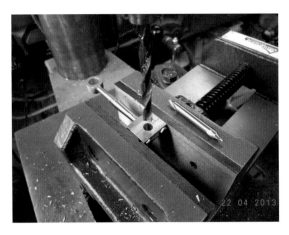

Drilling bearing brasses to take crank shaft.

by drilling the two 2.7 clearance holes at 12mm apart for both brasses and cut off over length from the bar. Next, bolt lightly to the connecting rod and tap them so that they level up, tighten the bolts good and tight, and file off the excess material. Mark the centre line, and set up level in the vice, and on the split line centre drill then a 5.5mm pilot drill. Finish off with a 6mm drill. Don't get too hung up about getting the 60mm hole centres spot on – it will tolerate a couple of millimetres error either way, and if you don't get the 6mm hole dead centre in the brasses you can always file them slightly bell mouth, so they will fit round the crank shaft.

Bearing Cap Part H23

This is a simple part made from a bit of 1/8" mild steel plate.

Piston and Cross Head Assembly Part H13

The piston and piston rod have already been dealt with previously.

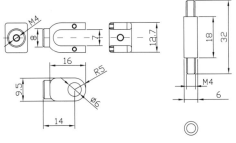

Part No H16:- Cross Head 1 off:- Material Mild Steel

Part No H18:- Cross Head Pin 1 Off:- Material Silver Steel

Part H16 Cross head part H18 cross head pin.

Cross Head Part H16

Made from 3/8"x 1/2" mild steel bar, mark its centre on the end of the bar and put in a small centre pop. Set it up true in the independent four-jaw using a wobble bar – the same as you did for the valve chest. Then, turn the small step in the end and drill and tap M4, keeping it on the bar as it makes it easier to grip. Mark out the centre lines on both faces and the position of the 6mm cross hole and the forked end. Over on the drill machine, first drill the 6mm cross hole. If you do this second, you will find the drill will kick over

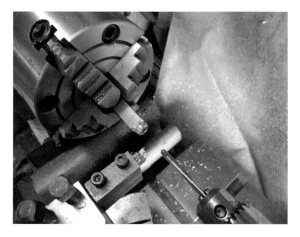

Turning drilling and tapping Cross head. Note use of four jaw to hold square bar.

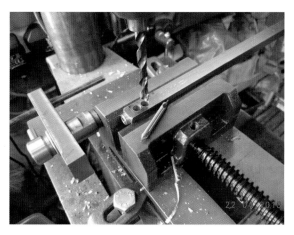

Drilling cross holes. Note part kept on the bar to assist clamping.

and you end up with a dog's dinner. How do I know this? Well, I made the dog's dinner! Next, chain drill out for the forked end. You can now cut it off the bar and, using files with the aid of a filing button, finish it off to shape.

Cross Head Pin Part H18

I made this from silver steel, and it is a simple enough part. Just clock the bar true before turning each end down and threading M4 with a die.

Slide Bar Part H17

Made from ¼" square brass, mark out the centre line on the bar, and using the sticky pin method line up on its centre. Clamp the vice to the table, and centre drill and tap M4. This is another tapping job where it's important to tap square. This time, I clamped the tap wrench tight onto the body of the tap close to the threads then gripped the tap lightly in the chuck, just enough to keep

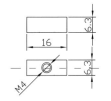

Part No H17 Slide Bar
2 off:- Material Mild
Steel

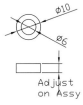

Part No H19 Thrust
Washer 2 off:-
Material Brass

Part H17 Slide bar part H19 thrust washer.

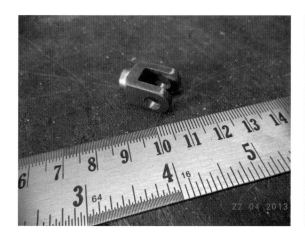

Completed cross head.

Drilling slide bars.

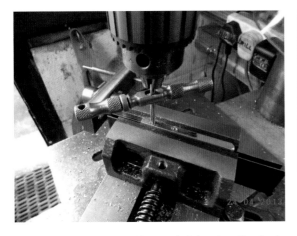

Tapping slide bars square. Note tap lightly gripped in chuck and wrench clamped on tap.

Completed connecting rod, cross head, slide bars and pin.

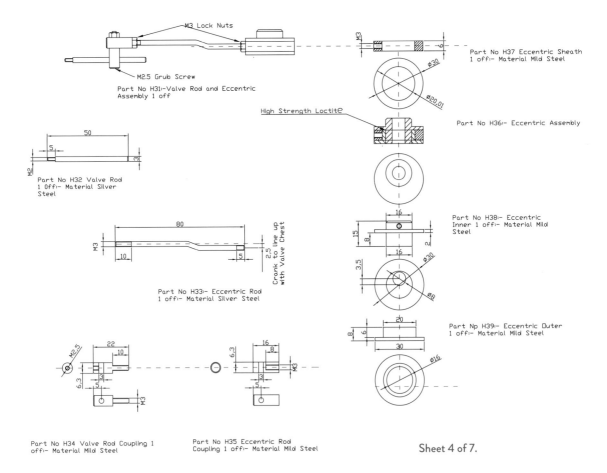

M3 Lock Nuts

M2.5 Grub Screw

Part No H31:-Valve Rod and Eccentric Assembly 1 off

Part No H32 Valve Rod 1 Off:- Material Silver Steel

High Strength Loctite

Crank to line up with Valve Chest

Part No H33:- Eccentric Rod 1 off:- Material Silver Steel

Part No H37 Eccentric Sheath 1 off:- Material Mild Steel

Part No H36:- Eccentric Assembly

Part No H38:- Eccentric Inner 1 off:- Material Mild Steel

Part Np H39:- Eccentric Outer 1 off:- Material Mild Steel

Part No H34 Valve Rod Coupling 1 off:- Material Mild Steel

Part No H35 Eccentric Rod Coupling 1 off:- Material Mild Steel

Sheet 4 of 7.

it square but not to stop it from turning. This way the tap will start square. Don't unclamp the vice from the table; just loosen the jaws and slide the bar along to the position for the next part. I have a set of thin parallels which makes this easy. The next best thing is to lightly grip the bar in the vice and put a flat piece of

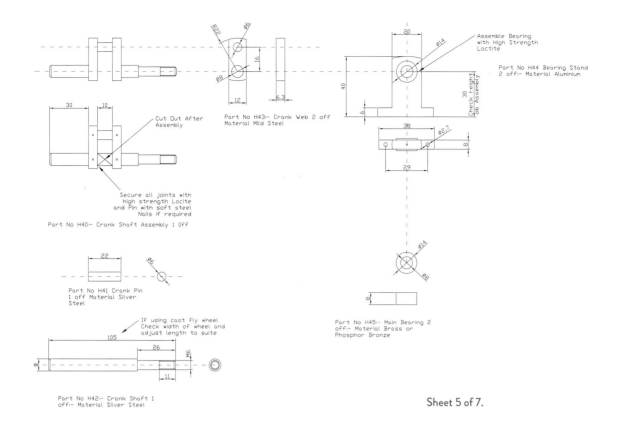

Part No H43:- Crank Web 2 off
Material Mild Steel

Part No H40:- Crank Shaft Assembly 1 Off

Cut Out After Assembly

Secure all joints with high strength Loctite and Pin with soft steel Nails if required

Part No H41 Crank Pin 1 off Material Silver Steel

If using cast fly wheel Check width of wheel and adjust length to suite

Part No H42:- Crank Shaft 1 off:- Material Silver Steel

Assemble Bearing with High Strength Loctite

Part No H44 Bearing Stand 2 off:- Material Aluminium

Check height ob Assembly

Part No H45:- Main Bearing 2 off:- Material Brass or Phosphor Bronze

plate on top of it. Lightly tap the plate to bring the part level with the top of the jaws, drill and tap for the second part. By not moving the vice you ensure that the hole is the same distance from the edge for both parts.

Bearing Stand Part H44

The bearing stands on the original engine have split bearing inclined a 45 degree to the base. This is done so that the thrust from the engine doesn't act along the line of the split and increase the rate of wear. I thought making split bearings and stands was an unnecessary complication, so I decided to take a liberty with the design and opt for a solid one-piece design, thus simplifying things considerably.

The stand is made from 5/16" x 1½" mild steel bar. This is another between-centres turning job, so cut two pieces off the bar 45mm long, clean up the cut edge with the file and mark and centre drill both ends. Then, using a driving plate or the four-jaw chuck, start by facing up one end off square, clean the pip back with a file, swap it round and turn the step back and

face off to 40mm length, and cut the pip off. This could be done with a hacksaw and files, if you wish, but I think this method gives a neater result.

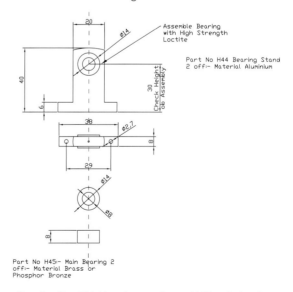

Assemble Bearing with High Strength Loctite

Part No H44 Bearing Stand 2 off:- Material Aluminium

Check Height ob Assembly

Part No H45:- Main Bearing 2 off:- Material Brass or Phosphor Bronze

Drawing Part **H44** bearing stand, part **H45** main bearing.

Turning bearing stand between centres.

Measuring centre height of cylinder using packing block and feeler gauges.

Vice stop parts.

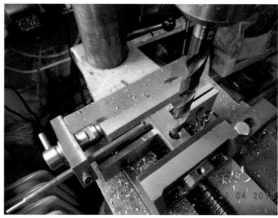

Using vice stop to ensure holes drilled at exactly the height.

Vice stopped screwed into side of vice.

The next operation starts to bring into play the vice stop. This is my interpretation of this particular bit of kit, and I use the same stop for my drill and mill vices. First, we have to measure the actual centre height of the cylinder bore with it sitting on the base. I have a digital height gauge for this, but I realize most of you won't have this option. I tried a number of alternative methods, and found the best method is to use a spacer and feeler gauges under the piston rod. With a little bit of maths, the result is as good as using the height gauge but a lot more fiddly. So, with the centre height determined, mark the centre height onto the bearing stand, clamp the stand in the drill vice with its base up against the fixed jaw, and set the vice stop up against the edge. Mark the edge that sits against the stop with a small centre pop, so you can keep them in the same orientation as they were drilled. This will help to keep everything lined up. Clamp the vice to the table and centre, put through a 10mm pilot drill and follow up with the 14mm finishing drill. Keep the vice clamped to the table and repeat with the second stand that should be identical in height to the first.

Mark the position of the 2x2.7 base holes and position in the drill vice. Set the vice stop and clamp the vice to the table and centre drill the first hole. Turn the part round and set against the stop and drill the second. Put it to one side and repeat with the second base, all without moving the stop or the vice. Job done! At this point I departed from drawing a little; I fancied giving the tops of the stands a radius so I did this using a filing button.

Main Bearings Part H45

This is a simple turning job. I made both bearings together, turning the outside diameter to a tight fit in the stands, drilling the bore then part the bearings off. They are fixed in the stand with bearing fit Loctite.

Completed bearing stands with bearings fitted.

Slide Bars Part H26

These are made from ¼" square mild steel bar. Cut them to length leaving 3mm on for finishing and face one end off in the lathe. Stand them on end and mark them off to all the same length. When making multiple parts like this, it helps to start with the parts all the

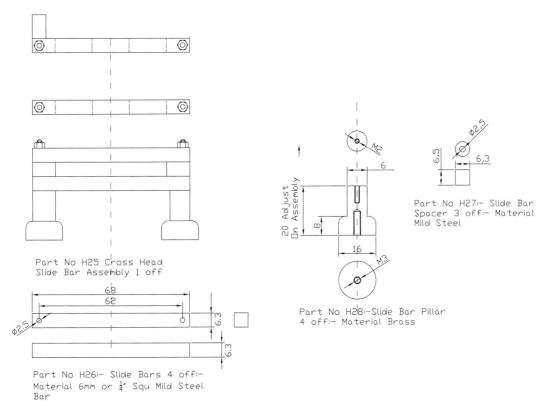

Part H25 Cross head slide bar assembly.

Using vice stop to drill slide bars.

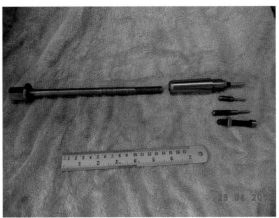

Parts for lathe back stop.

same size, so I then faced the other end off to bring them all to the same length. With them all the same length, you can now take advantage of the vice stop. Mark the centre line on one bar and the position for one hole. Line this up in the drill, set the vice stop and clamp the vice to the table and drill it through. Swap it around and drill the other end. Repeat for the rest of the bars. They should all end up with a hole at the same distance apart.

Slide Bar Spacer Valve Rod Guide Part H29

Whilst you've got the drill vice set up, now is the time to make the slide bar spacer and valve rod guide. This is made from ¼" square brass. Just stick a length of bar in the vice and drill one of the 3mm holes through. The other hole will be spotted through when you've got a bit more of the assembly done, so put this part safely to one side.

Slide Bar Pillar Part H28

Now is the time to introduce you to another useful stop, a chuck back stop. The parts can be made without it, but this will entail a lot of taking the parts in and out and measuring. But it's up to you how you do it. My back stop is simply a draw bar with an M3 morse taper mandrel tapped M8 to take different sizes of stops. I make these as I require them.

The slide bar pillars have to be the correct height to bring the slide bars to the correct position for the cross head. This can be worked out from the thicknesses of the slide bars and the cylinder centre height

Lathe back stop fitted into head stock. Chuck removed for clarity.

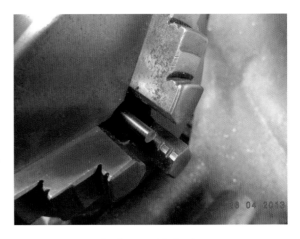

Back stop with chuck.

you used for the bearing stands. The pillars need to be all the same height. This is where the back stop comes in handy.

I made my pillars from a length of ¼" hex bar, but any suitable size bar will do. Just chuck up face and drill and tap one end M3 and part off to length, leaving 1mm on for finishing. Make four of these.

Fit the back stop, push one of the pillars up against the back stop and take a light skim off it. Remove and measure, put it back against the back stop and face off to size. Zero your dials and lock the saddle. Now all you have to do is put each in turn up against the stop and face off. They should all come out the same. Drill and tap M2.5.

Slide Bar Spacers Part H27

This a similar job to making the pillars that again uses the back stop.

Base Plate Part H53

We are getting to the stage now when we will need the base. I don't like to finish the base off at one go, I prefer to drill and fit parts as they are ready for assembly. The base is one of those parts where errors on parts start to combine and can have quite a big effect on where they are to be finally positioned. It's far better to assemble parts where they do their job best.

The base was made from a piece of ¼"x 3" wide aluminium plate bought on the internet. It was a bit wider than required but it was the best I could get. If you're unable to find a suitable piece of aluminium, a piece of medium density fibreboard (MDF) will be perfectly acceptable and after a lick of paint no one will be any the wiser. The first job was to cut it off to the correct width. I used the top of the vice jaw as a guide for the saw to keep things reasonably straight. I then set too with a file and a straight edge to bring it reasonably straight and square.

The first part to be positioned is the cylinder assembly. I just located the position by marking round the base with a felt tip. I then scribed a centre line down

Sawing base to size. Note use of vice to keep cut straight.

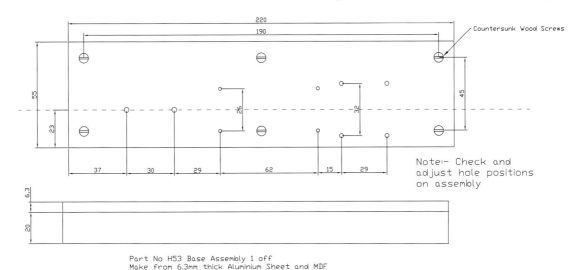

Part No H53 Base Assembly 1 off
Make from 6.3mm thick Aluminium Sheet and MDF

Part H53 base plate.

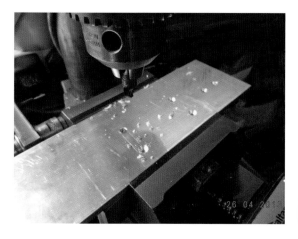

Drill and countersink base plate after checking hole position.

Spotting through valve rod guide position.

its length and drilled the fixing holes on this line and countersunk them. With the cylinder fixed to the base plate, try a loose assemble to see how it looks, and to find the best position for the slide bars. Mark the base plate, drill and counter sink for M3 countersunk cap screws.

With the slide bars in place, it's time to finish of the slide bar spacer and valve rod guide part H29. It's important that the holes to guide the valve rod line up. So, on the end of a bit of 3mm steel, turn up a cone to make a transfer punch. Put this through the valve rod guide from the back of the valve chest and give it a light biff so that it marks the part. On the mark, drill through 3mm. It should now line up perfectly. Note: you will have to put a piece of drinks-can shim under this part on assembly to allow free movement of the cross head. You can now fit the valve chest end plate part, fixing it in place with some super glue.

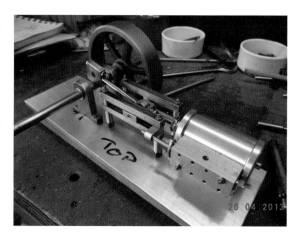

Trail assembly of parts.

Valve rod and eccentric assembly part H31

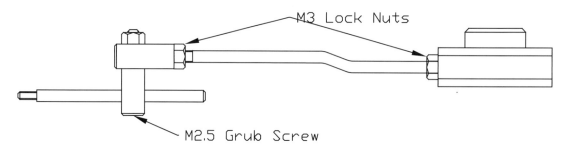

Part H31 Valve rod and eccentric assembly.

Valve Rod Part H32

This has been dealt with previously.

Part No H32 Valve Rod
1 Off:- Material Silver
Steel

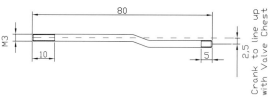

Part No H33:- Eccentric Rod
1 off:- Material Silver Steel

Part H32 Valve rod part H33 eccentric rod.

Eccentric Rod Part H33

Made from a length of 3mm silver steel, cut off a generous length and thread both ends M3. Bend the offset in the vice, making final adjustments to the length and offset at final assembly.

Valve Rod Coupling Part H34

Made from 1.4 inch diameter stainless steel, the part calls for a 3mm cross hole. The simplest way to do this is to first make a thick guide bush with a 3mm hole in it from the same bit of bar you are going to use for the part. Then all you have to do is place the bush on

Using a drill bush to drill through the exact centre of the bar.

Drill bush and part.

the bar, clamp the two together in the drill vice and use the bush to guide the drill across the centre of the

Part No H34 Valve Rod Coupling 1 off:- Material Mild Steel

Part No H35 Eccentric Rod Coupling 1 off:- Material Mild Steel

Part H34 valve rod coupling part H35

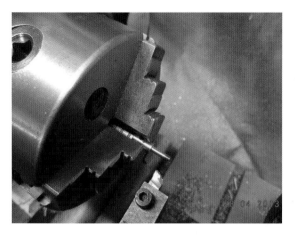

Turn and thread with a die.

Assembled coupling.

bar. It is now a simple job to cut the part off the bar and to turn and thread the other end.

Eccentric Rod Coupling Part H35

This is also made from ¼ inch diameter stainless steel, in a similar way to the valve rod coupling.

Eccentric Assembly Part H36

The Eccentric is a three-part assembly held together with high strength Loctite 603. This allows all the parts to be finish-turned in the lathe.

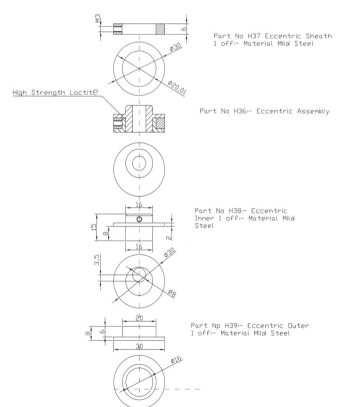

Part H36 eccentric assembly.

Eccentric Sheath Part H37

I was lucky to have some 28mm OD x 20mm ID 70/30 brass tube in my scrap box that was ideal for the job. It was a little under drawing size on the OD but this could be tolerated. It was a simple matter of parting the tube off to length and drilling and tapping M3. But if you are making from solid bar, you will have to face, skim up the diameter to size, centre drill and drill and finally bore out to size before parting off and drilling and tapping the M3 hole.

Eccentric Outer Part H39

It's best to make the eccentric outer first as it is easier to fit a shaft to a bore than a bore to a shaft. The part is made from a stub end of 32mm diameter mild steel. Face off centre drill, then put down a couple of

Turn diameter and step to size.

Eccentric sheath parted off.

Face off to size.

Boring out the eccentric outer.

roughing drills. Then, with a boring bar, bore out to 16mm diameter. You can measure the bore with your digital callipers but remember the legs of the callipers have flats on them so you will get a false reading. The bore will be actually bigger than the callipers are telling you, so aim for a calliper reading of about 15.8mm. Next, turn the 20mm diameter to give a nice running fit on the bore of the sheath. Make the 6mm length about 0.1mm longer than the width of the sheath, swap it round in the chuck and face the other end off to length.

Eccentric Inner Part H38

Again, made from a stub end of 32mm mild steel, start by facing off and skimming up the OD, then turn the 16mm diameter for a nice push fit on the eccentric

Trial assembly of parts.

Eccentric parts ready for assembly using Loctite.

Marking out the eccentric throw.

Accurately position throw using independent four jaw, wobble bar and dial test indicator.

outer. The picture shows a trial assembly of the part on the lathe. Swap it round in the lathe and face off to length and put in a small centre mark. Using the centre mark, scribe a 7mm diameter arc and put a small centre pop anywhere on this arc to mark the throw of the eccentric. Using the four-jaw chuck and the wobble bar trick. Clock the throw up, centre drill followed by a roughing drill then an 8mm reamer or, if no reamer is available, an 8mm drill. Finish off by turning the 16mm diameter, and drilling and tapping for the M3 fixing grub screw. The whole assembly is put together with high strength Loctite 603. Don't forget to put the eccentric sleeve in place, and to avoid contaminating the sleeve with adhesive (so it doesn't rotate) put a few drops of the adhesive into the bore. That way, any surplus is pushed to the outside, out of harm's way. If you do have a disaster, keep calm and don't panic. The adhesive bond is easily broken by applying a little heat. This is best done with one of those hot air paint stripping guns.

Crank Shaft Assembly Part H40

The crank shaft is a steel fabrication, with the webs glued and pinned onto the shaft.

Crank Pin Part H41

The crank pin is just a 22mm length of 6mm diameter silver steel.

Crank Shaft Part H42

This is a piece of 8mm silver steel, just cut off to length. Face both ends and clock the piece true in

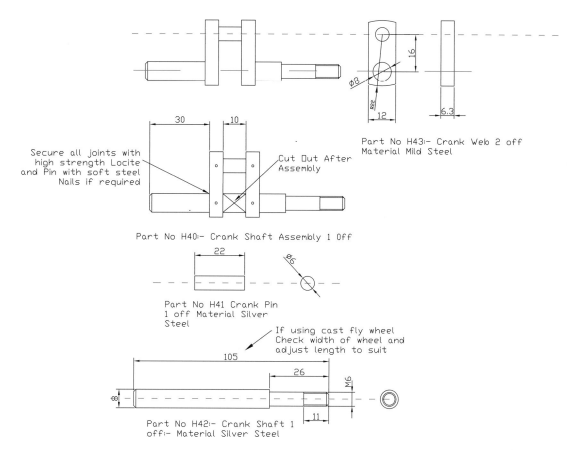

30 10

Secure all joints with
high strength Locite
and Pin with soft steel
Nails if required

Cut Out After
Assembly

Part No H40:- Crank Shaft Assembly 1 Off

22

Ø6

Part No H41 Crank Pin
1 off Material Silver
Steel

Part No H43:- Crank Web 2 off
Material Mild Steel

Ø3
R22
16
12
6.3

If using cast fly wheel
Check width of wheel and
adjust length to suit

105

26

Ø8
M6
11

Part No H42:- Crank Shaft 1
off:- Material Silver Steel

Part H40 crank shaft assembly.

the chuck. Turn one end down to 6mm diameter and thread M6 with a die.

Note: if you are using a cast flywheel, you may have to increase the length of this part.

Turn and thread crank shaft. Note die holder.

Crank Webs Part H43

The webs are made from 1/4" x 1/2" mild steel bar. Cut two pieces off the bar, allowing a couple of mm on each face for finishing. Mark the centre of the bar and the position for the shafts. It pays to have an appreciation of how a part functions and what the important features are that make it function correctly. It's not always obvious what the really critical features are; people have a tendency to focus on the feature that is easy to measure. In the case of the web, you might think that getting the hole centres exactly 16mm is important, but in fact the really important feature is to get the holes centred in both webs exactly the same. They can be out by up to 0.5mm without having any functional effect, but they must be both the same. If they are not the same, things will be twisted out of line and the engine will be tight and not run. Having this understanding helps to simplify their manufacture: all you have to do is first drill an 8mm hole in each web, then to tie the two webs together with a little stub of

Webs marked out.

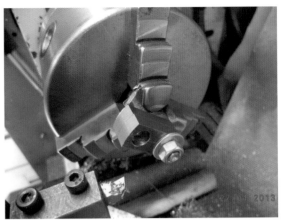

Radius webs on lathe using a mandrel.

Drilling webs. Note webs pinned together for drilling second hole to ensure a perfect matching pair.

Completed webs.

Checking webs exactly match with two rods.

8mm bar, and then drill the second 6mm hole through both webs. The hole centres must come out exactly the same in each web. The centres for mine came out as 16.3mm which means the engine will have a stroke of 32.6mm which is easily accommodated within the length of the cylinder.

To finish off we now have to tidy up the ends. First, turn up an 8mm diameter mandrel with a M6 thread. Bolt the webs to this and, with light cuts, clean up the first end to give a nice arc. Then turn the mandrel down to 6mm and do the same for the other end of the webs.

Assembling the Crank Shaft

The crank shaft is first assembled using high strength Loctite 603. This grade gives you twenty to thirty seconds before it goes off, so you have time to get things positioned correctly – but you will find it easier if you do it in stages. Dry assemble the shaft and first apply the adhesive to the crank pin. Line up the ends with the webs and let it go off, then apply the adhesive to the shaft. Get it in the correct position and let it go off. This way you have less of a juggling act to do. Let the adhesive cure for a good twenty-four hours to come to full strength. As well as the adhesive, I like the added security of pinning the webs to the shaft. For the pins, I use soft mild steel wood nails. Just lightly grip the assembly in the drill vice and drill straight through the web and shaft. Add a small chamfer to either end of the hole, remove the head off the nail, tap through the hole and lightly peen the end to spread the nail into the chamfer.

Clean up with a file. You can now cut away the part of the shaft between the webs to complete the crank shaft.

With the crank shaft complete, you can now use it to get everything in position to drill the bedplate for the bearing stands. Whilst I was doing this, I had one of those senior moments: I lost one of the bearing stands. After a frantic search, I resorted to tidying the work area up – nothing. I brushed the floor – nothing. I'd gone from anger at my stupidity to despair. So, I enlisted the help of my boss to do a forensic search of my shed. 'This is what we are looking for,' I said, pointing. 'There are three of them?' she said. 'No, just two,' I said a little tetchily. 'Well, there's two there,' she said, pointing. Can you find the missing part? (It's on the end of the crank shaft.)

Crank shaft glued using Loctite.

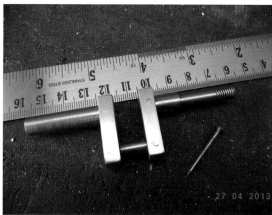

Cut away centre to completed crankshaft.

Adding the braces. Drilling and pinning with soft nails.

Can you find the missing part?

Flywheel Part H46 or H47

Here you have a choice: you can either fabricate a flywheel or purchase a cast iron STUART type flywheel. I get my cast flywheels from RDG (usual disclaimer). They are quite reasonably priced and of good quality. If you are using a cast flywheel, check its width and make any adjustments to the length of the crank shaft to ensure that it overhangs the base.

To machine up the cast flywheel, first give the flywheel a good going over with a file removing any flashing and nasty bits, and check for blow holes. These usually machine out. Any that are left, if not in

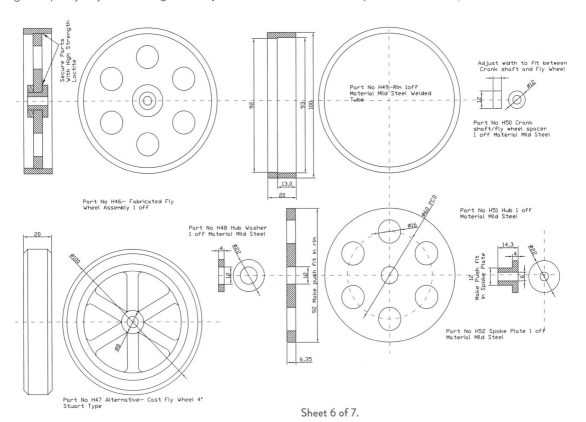

Part No H46:- Fabricated Fly Wheel Assembly 1 off

Part No H48 Hub Washer 1 off Material Mild Steel

Part No H49:-Rim 1off Material Mild Steel Welded Tube

Adjust width to fit between Crank shaft and Fly Wheel

Part No H50 Crank shaft/fly wheel spacer 1 off Material Mild Steel

Part No H51 Hub 1 off Material Mild Steel

Make Push fit in Spoke Plate

Part No H52 Spoke Plate 1 off Material Mild Steel

Part No H47 Alternative:- Cast Fly Wheel 4' Stuart Type

Sheet 6 of 7.

Machining cast flywheel in four jaw chuck.

Clocking flywheel up true with DTI for finishing.

Completed cast flywheel.

a critical area, can be filled, but if they are a problem get your supplier to change it.

Mount it in the four-jaw chuck and get the inside rim running as true as you can. Then skim up a register on the OD, face off and clean up the hub and the inside of the rim. If there are hard spots in the casting, you may have to use a tungsten tool. Don't take a too-light first cut; it has to be a deep heavy cut to get under the hard scaled surface. Flip it round and, gripping on the inside of the rim, clock the OD register up true. Clean the OD and face, clean up the hub and inside of the rim and chamfer the edges. Put in a nice deep centre followed by a 5.5mm roughing drill and, if you have one, a 6mm reamer. If not, use a 6mm drill.

Fabricated Flywheel Assembly Part H46

A fabricated flywheel will look more like the flywheel on the original engine. It doesn't have spokes, just

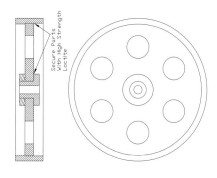

Part H46 fabricated flywheel.

four holes through the webbing. I think this is an unusual feature for an engine of this time, and it set me off wondering if this is not the original flywheel but something the Bolton lads knocked up for it. The flywheel is held together with high strength Loctite 603, I've used this method on quite a few flywheels now, and it seems to stand the test of time as I have had no trouble with any of them. (I have since confirmed that the flywheel was indeed knocked up by the Bolton lads as the original was missing.)

Flywheel Rim Part H49

The rim is made from 100mm diameter by 4mm thick wall, welded mild steel tube. I found a cut off for sale on the internet, and it seems to come in two wall thickness (3mm or 4mm). I opted for the thicker 4mm. Cut a 25mm sliver off the pipe using a hacksaw, then

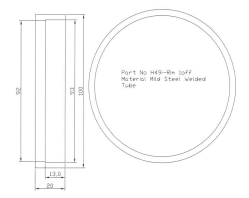

Part H49 flywheel rim.

Skimming up welded steel tube for flywheel rim. Note three jaw gripping on the inside of the tube.

Boring step in rim.

Drilling spoke plate.

gripping it on its inside in the three-jaw chuck, face off the rough edge. Flip it round and grip it in the same way, but this time try and get it running as true as you can. Being a welded tube, it's all shapes and you will not get it perfect. The key here is to get it so that it least offends the eye. Face it up to width and skim up the OD. In the four-jaw chuck, grip it on the OD, clock it as true as you can, and with a boring bar clean the bore up to a length of 13mm so that you have a step for the spoke plate to butt up against. Clean any remaining weld splatter away with a file.

Spoke Plate Part H52

This is made from a 100mm x 100mm x 1/4" thick hot rolled mild steel plate, again from the internet. Mark the centre and scribe a 100mm diameter circle, the 60mm PCD and the position for the 16mm diameter holes. Trim the corners away with a hacksaw. Clamp

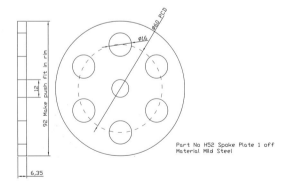

Part H52 spoke plate.

Skim spoke plate diameter for close fit in rim.

firmly to the drill table, use a deep centre drill followed by a roughing drill and then a ½" finishing drill. Turn up a mandrel on the lathe that's a nice push fit in the ½" hole and bolt the plate securely to it. Then, with a sharp tool, nibble the plate down to a diameter, that's a nice push fit into the rim. Finish off by drilling the 6 x 16mm holes. I drilled 4 x 22 holes because the flywheel on the original has four holes, but the 22mm drill made my old drilling machine grunt somewhat, so 16mm holes will be easier. It's up to you which size you go with.

Hub Part H51: Hub Spacer Part 48: Crank Shaft/Flywheel Spacer

These three parts are all made from mild steel. The hub is made to a tight fit in the spoke plate. The hub spacer is made to a tight fit on the hub, whilst the

Part No H48 Hub Washer
1 off Material Mild Steel

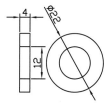

Adjust width to fit between
Crank shaft and Fly Wheel

12

Ø12

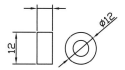

Part No H50 Crank
shaft/fly wheel spacer
I off Material Mild Steel

Part No H51 Hub 1 off
Material Mild Steel

14,3

4

Ø22

Make Push fit
in Spoke Plate

12

6

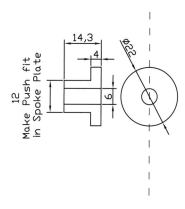

Part H48 hub washer; part H50 crank shaft/flywheel spacer; part H51 hub.

flywheel spacer fits on the crank shaft, to position the flywheel.

Completing the Flywheel

Assemble the spoke plate to the rim using Loctite 603. From the same side, assemble the hub again with 603, curing off in a warm room for a good twenty-four hours. Then assemble the hub washer and let these cure off. With the adhesive well cured, grip the flywheel by the hub in the three-jaw chuck so that you will be pushing onto the step you turned in the rim. True the rim up as best as you can so that it is not too offensive to the eye, put in a good deep centre, followed by a 5.5mm drill and finish with a 6mm reamer or a 6mm drill.

Assemble rim, spoke plate and hub with Loctite.

Clock flywheel assembly up true and drill and ream hub.

Setting the Engine Up for First Run

That's all of the parts made, so before you go ahead and put the finishing touches to the engine, it is time to see if it will run. Pack the cylinder, piston rod gland and the valve gland with either graphite packing, or PTFE tape (the sort that plumbers use). Simply twist it into a string and use it as packing, but whichever method you use don't make the mistake of packing too tight. Seal the front and rear covers to the cylinder using gasket sealant or even bathroom sealant. Try to see if it will turn over fairly easily by hand; if it won't you have to

Using PTFE tape to pack valve gland.

chase out any tight spots. A good trick is to loosen all the fixings off, then part by part start to tighten everything up. If you feel the engine go tight, investigate that part and make adjustments to correct it. This may mean using shim, or polishing with emery cloth or even taking a file to it. Work methodically and think about what you are doing. This is the time when you really get to understand an engine. When you are satisfied you have it turning over freely you can set the valve events.

The engines are designed for running on compressed air fed by any small compressor, though they are perfectly capable of running on steam but this would require a boiler and making a boiler is a subject all on its own.

Setting the Valve Events

The first thing you have to do is centralize the valve travel. The easiest way to do this is by having the eccentric loose on the crank shaft. With the eccentric at the 12 o'clock position, bring the valve rod coupling into the mid position between the valve chest and the slide bar spacer and nip it up. Rotate the eccentric 360 degrees to check that the coupling has free movement. Make adjustments as required which may mean taking a file to some of the parts. To centralize the movement of the valve, again with the

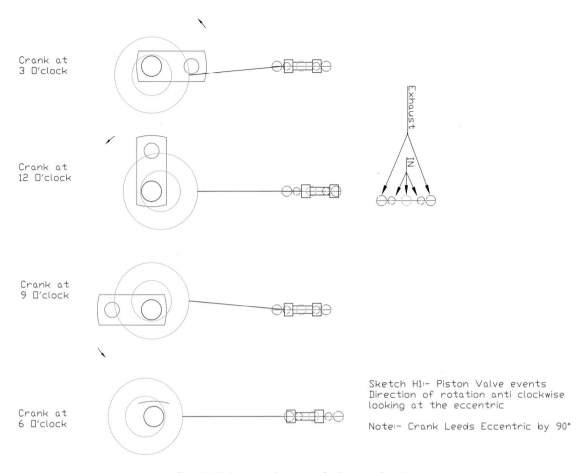

Crank at
3 O'clock

Crank at
12 O'clock

Exhaust

IN

Crank at
9 O'clock

Crank at
6 O'clock

Sketch H1:- Piston Valve events
Direction of rotation anti clockwise
looking at the eccentric

Note:- Crank Leeds Eccentric by 90°

Sketch H1 showing valve events for horizontal engine.

eccentric loose on the crank shaft, rotate and observe the movement of the piston valve down the inlet hole. Adjust the valve rod in or out on the coupling until you equalize the movement of the valve. With this done, you can now set the valve timing. The eccentric is 90 degrees behind the crank, so with the crank at the 12 o'clock position the eccentric will be at the 3 o'clock position. Looking through the air inlet, you should see the piston valve covering half the hole. Nip up the grub screw to secure the eccentric to the crank shaft, as you don't want it to slip.

Give everything a good dose of oil, couple it up to the air supply and give it a blast. With a bit of luck it should run with no trouble. At first keep it generously supplied with oil until you have it run in. Mine will run at 10 psi at about 100 rpm if I give it full pressure. At 60 psi it will rip along at 1400 rpm. Now is the time to

show your handy work to the wife and kids, brothers and sisters, grandads, grandmas, aunties and uncles, the dog, the cat and all and sundry. And to have a well-earned grin on your face.

Finishing Off

To do the engine justice you now need to finish it off, and turn it from just an engine into a very nice engine. The first thing I did with mine was to re-sculpt the bedplate, cutting out radiuses around the bolt down holes and adding thick aluminium washers so that it looked more like a cast base. I can remember seeing a horizontal beam engine at Stott Park Bobbin Mill (in the Lake District) which was mounted on a sandstone plinth and thought it would be interesting to try and model this. Two pieces of ½" thick chipboard were cut to the same size, and I then rounded all the edges off with a file, and added a series of grooves spaced around the edge to represent the courses of stone. This was then stained with water soluble wood stain to represent my local Cheshire red sandstone, and the surface sealed off with a watered-down wash from PVA adhesive. The result was quite pleasing with the chipboard giving it quite a realistic stone textured finish.

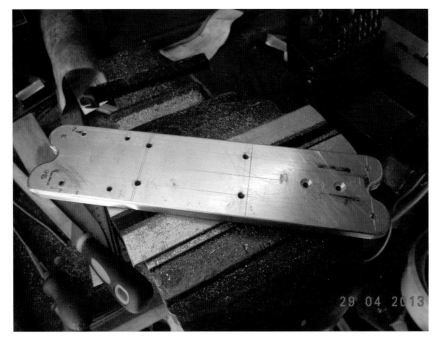

Spruced up base plate.

Plinth made from coarse chip board.

Stains and PVA.

Stained and completed plinth simulating sandstone.

Painting is something I struggle with. I always seem to end up with runs, no matter how hard I try to avoid them. Though far from perfect, my paint jobs just about pass muster. I just have to keep trying to improve. Strip the engine down and give all the parts a good going over. Paint doesn't like sharp corners and has a tendency to pull away from them, so round these off. Rough up surfaces to be painted to give the paint a key, and thoroughly de-grease all parts. I have a small, cheap ultrasonic cleaner for small parts.

Bigger parts get a ride in the dishwasher. Give all the parts a good wash and scrub in hot water to get rid of any residue from the de-greasing operation and allow to dry off overnight. Mask off the area not being painted.

I apply the paint from spray cans, and I always use them outside. I hang the painted parts on S hooks inside the garage roof to dry off. The non-ferrous parts get an undercoat of etch primer. This needs to be left for twenty-four hours to do its job. The ferrous parts also get a suitable undercoat. Apply a number of thin topcoats, allow them to dry off between coats and leave for two or three days to completely harden off before the final assembly.

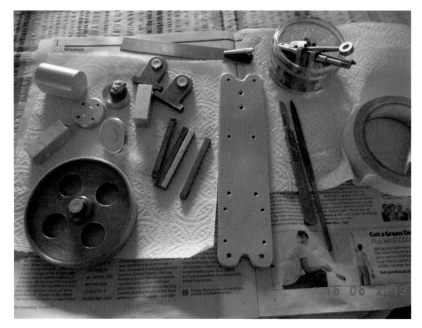

Parts prepared for painting.

Range of spray paints.

Coffee sticks glued on cotton cloth for cladding.

Clad cylinders.

The first engine that I build was Tubal Cain's Beam Engine Mary. I tried to add wooden cladding to the cylinder, but this was a complete disaster, and I gave up on it in the end. I have since found out how to do this, so I was keen to have a go on this engine. It's really quite simple once you know how. Stick some coffee stirrers to a piece of cotton cloth, using Copydex adhesive. This is a latex-based adhesive and is quite flexible. Give it plenty of time to dry off, then clean off any surplus adhesive, and stain. I watered down the same stain I used for the base and gave it a couple of coats of varnish. It is then a simple job to cut it to size (I used scissors for this) and to stick

to the cylinder with two-way sticky tape. Two brass bands were added held in place with 1/16" brass rivets, by drilling through into the cylinder and fixing the rivets with super glue. All that was required now was a nice hardwood base. Because of my allergy to hardwood, a friend makes these for me. The result is very pleasing.

That's the first engine completed. If you took on the challenge to make this engine, I hope you enjoyed the process. The next engine is slightly more of a challenge, but it should not pose too great a challenge to those who prefer to start with this engine.

5 Vertical Cross Single Component Manufacture

THE INSPIRATION FOR THE model is Bolton's Northern Mill Engine Society Kenyon engine. This is a vertical cross compound engine and is believed to be the only survivor of this type in the UK. The engine was removed in 1977 from Messrs Jonas Kenyon's Dearneside Mills in Denby Dale, near Huddersfield when the company closed. The original intention was to rebuild it in Yorkshire, but for various reasons this never happened, and the parts of the engine lay in various fields for thirty years. Eventually, when under threat of being scrapped, it was brought to Bolton in 2008 for the Bolton Society Members to renovate.

The original engine maker is unknown. It was rebuilt from earlier parts and installed at Dearneside Mills in about 1900 with the assistance of James Lumb & Sons of Elland, who were better known as makers of steam engine governors. It has a number of unusual features, including a special 'trip gear' (patented by James Lumb in 1892) operating a supplementary

The giant engine as displayed and run at Bolton's Northern Mill Engine Society.

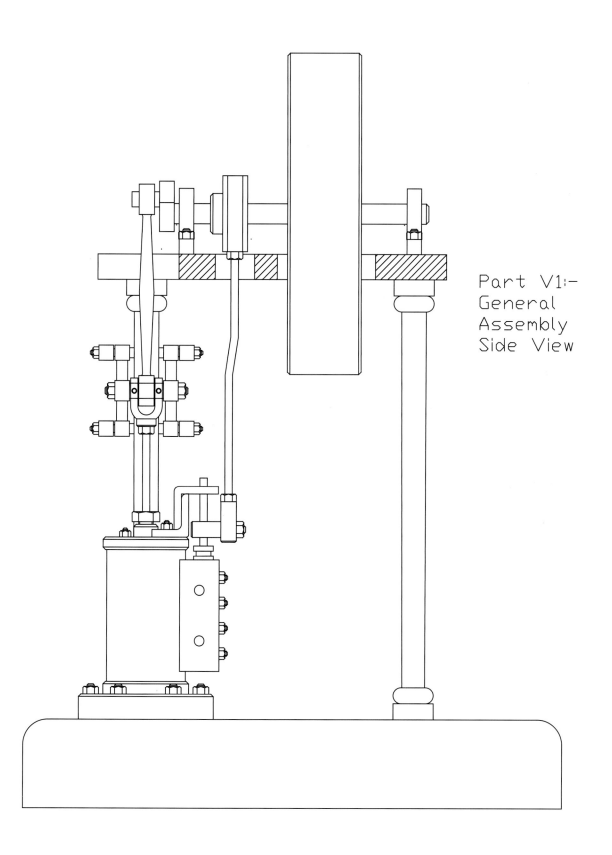

Part V1:-
General
Assembly
Side View

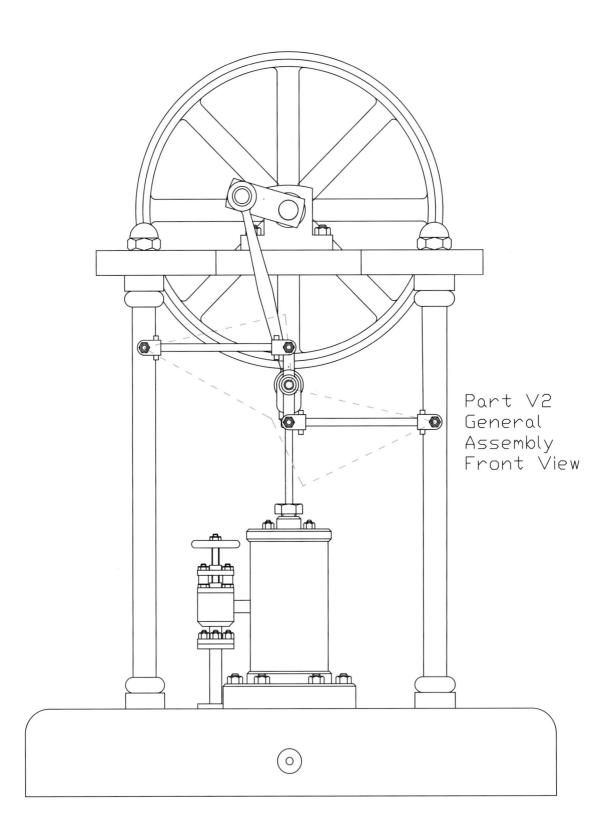

Part V2
General
Assembly
Front View

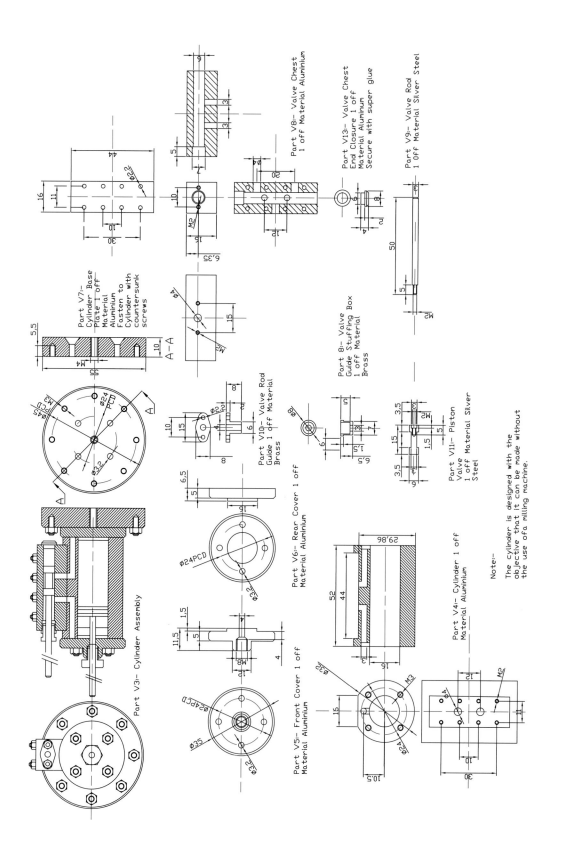

Part V8:- Valve Chest
1 off Material Aluminium

Part V13:- Valve Chest
End Closure 1 off
Material Aluminum
Secure with super glue

Part V9:- Valve Rod
1 Off Material Silver Steel

Part V7:- Cylinder Base
Plate 1 off
Material
Aluminium
Fasten to
Cylinder with
countersunk
screws

A–A

Part 8:- Valve
Guide Stuffing Box
1 off Material
Brass

Part V10:- Valve Rod
Guide 1 off Material
Brass

Part V11:- Piston
Valve
1 off Material Silver
Steel

Part V3:- Cylinder Assembly

Part V6:- Rear Cover 1 off
Material Aluminium

Part V5:- Front Cover 1 off
Material Aluminium

Part V4:- Cylinder 1 off
Material Aluminium

Note:-

The cylinder is designed with the
objective that it can be made without
the use of a milling machine.

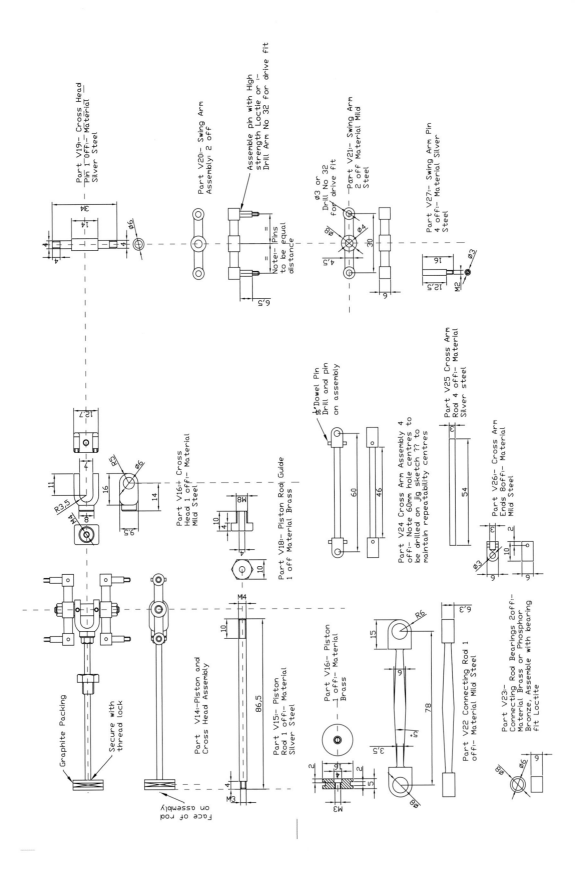

Part V19:- Cross Head Pin 1 off:- Material Silver Steel

Part V20:- Swing Arm Assembly: 2 off

Assemble pin with High strength Loctle or '- Drill Arm No 32 for drive fit

Note:- Pins to be equal distance

Ø3 or Drill No 32 for drive fit

Part V21:- Swing Arm 2 off Material Mild Steel

Part V27:- Swing Arm Pin 4 off:- Material Silver Steel

Dowel Pin Drill and pin on assembly

Part V24 Cross Arm Assembly 4 off:- Note 60mm hole centres to be drilled on Jig sketch ?? to maintain repeatability centres

Part V25 Cross Arm Rod 4 off:- Material Silver steel

Part V26:- Cross Arm Ends 8off:- Material Mild Steel

Part V16:+ Cross Head 1 off:- Material Mild Steel

Part V18:- Piston Rod Guide 1 off Material Brass

Graphite Packing

Secure with thread lock

Part V14:-Piston and Cross Head Assembly

Part V15:- Piston Rod 1 off:- Material Silver Steel

Face of rod on assembly

Part V16:- Piston 1 off:- Material Brass

Part V22 Connecting Rod 1 off:- Material Mild Steel

Part V23:- Connecting Rod Bearings 2off:- Material Brass or Phosphor Bronze, Assemble with bearing fit Loctite

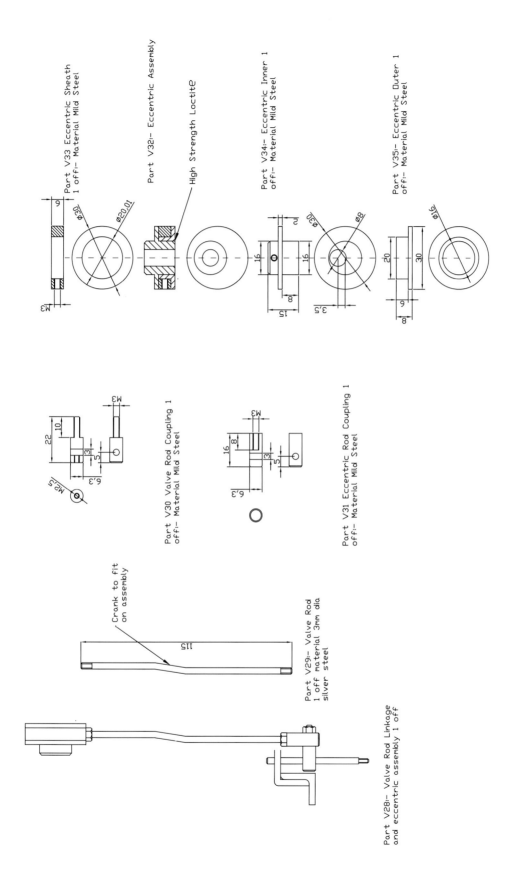

Part V33 Eccentric Sheath
1 off:- Material Mild Steel

Part V32:- Eccentric Assembly

High Strength Loctite

Part V34:- Eccentric Inner 1
off:- Material Mild Steel

Part V35:- Eccentric Outer 1
off:- Material Mild Steel

Part V30 Valve Rod Coupling 1
off:- Material Mild Steel

Part V31 Eccentric Rod Coupling 1
off:- Material Mild Steel

Crank to fit
on assembly

Part V29:- Valve Rod
1 off material 3mm dia
silver steel

Part V28:- Valve Rod Linkage
and eccentric assembly 1 off

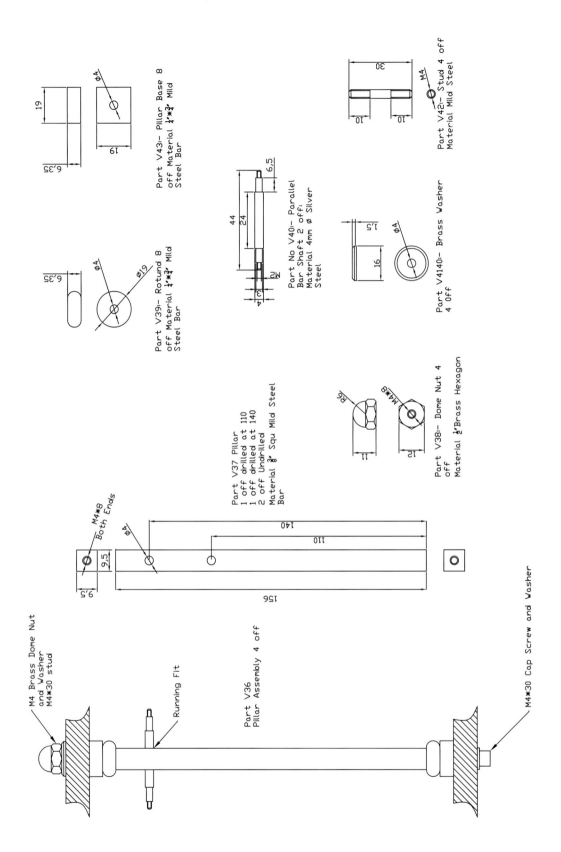

Part V43:- Pillar Base 8 off Material ¼"*¾" Mild Steel Bar

Part V42:- Stud 4 off Material Mild Steel

Part V39:- Rotund 8 off Material ¼"*¾" Mild Steel Bar

Part No V40:- Parallel Bar Shaft 2 off; Material 4mm Ø Silver Steel

Part V4140:- Brass Washer 4 0ff

Part V37 Pillar
1 off drilled at 110
1 off drilled at 140
2 off Undrilled
Material ⅜" Squ Mild Steel Bar

Part V38:- Dome Nut 4 off
Material ½" Brass Hexagon

M4*8 Both Ends

M4 Brass Dome Nut and Washer
M4*30 stud

Running Fit

Part V36
Pillar Assembly 4 off

M4*30 Cap Screw and Washer

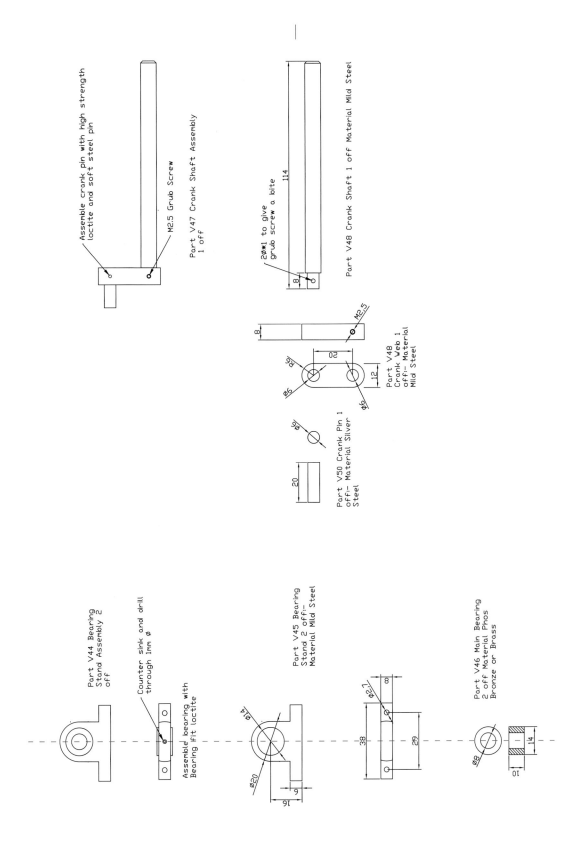

Assemble crank pin with high strength loctite and soft steel pin

M2.5 Grub Screw

Part V47 Crank Shaft Assembly 1 off

2Ø*1 to give grub screw a bite

114

8

Part V48 Crank Shaft 1 off Material Mild Steel

8

M2.5

R6

20

Ø6

12

Ø6

Part V48 Crank Web 1 off - Material Mild Steel

Ø6

20

Part V50 Crank Pin 1 off - Material Silver Steel

Part V44 Bearing Stand Assembly 2 off

Counter sink and drill through 1mm Ø

Assemble bearing with Bearing ifit loctite

Part V45 Bearing Stand 2 off - Material Mild Steel

Ø14

Ø20

16

9

Ø2.7

8

38

29

Part V46 Main Bearing 2 off Material Phos Bronze or Brass

Ø8

14

10

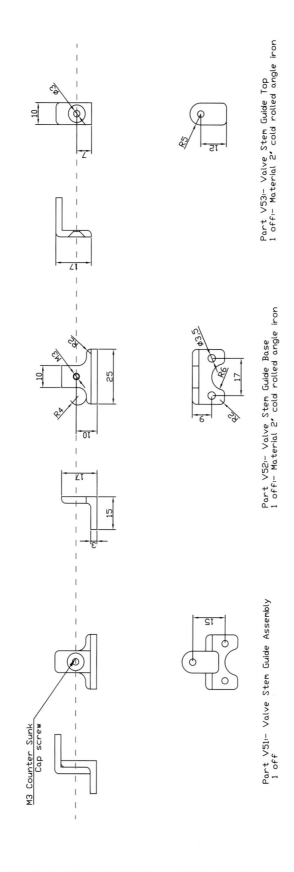

M3 Counter Sunk
Cap screw

Part V51:- Valve Stem Guide Assembly
1 off

Part V52:- Valve Stem Guide Base
1 off:- Material 2" cold rolled angle iron

Part V53:- Valve Stem Guide Top
1 off:- Material 2" cold rolled angle iron

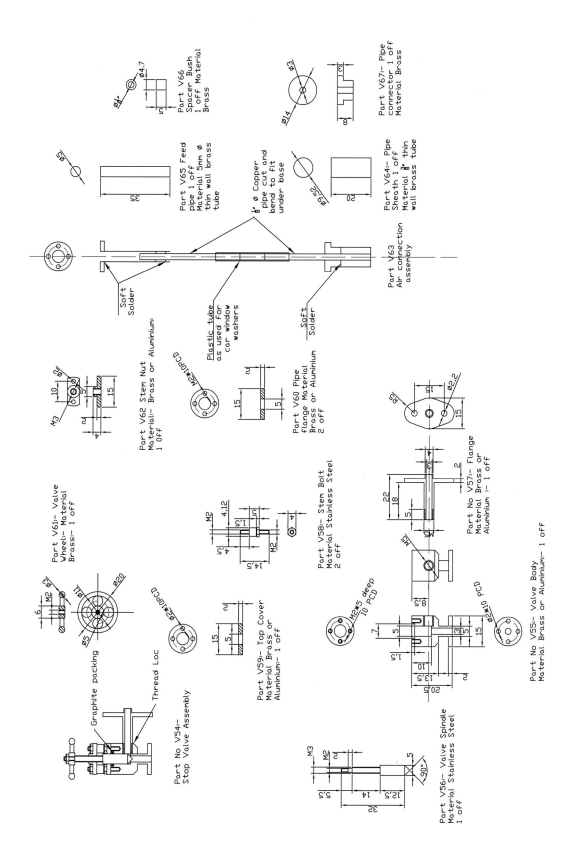

Ø4.7

Part V66 Spacer Bush 1 off Material Brass

Ø3

3

Part V67:- Pipe connector 1 off Material Brass

Ø14

8

Ø5

35

Part V65 Feed pipe 1 off Material 5mm Ø thin wall brass tube

⅛" Ø Copper pipe cut and bend to fit under base

Ø5.25

20

Part V64:- Pipe Sheath 1 off Material ⅜" thin wall brass tube

Part V63 Air connection assembly

Soft Solder

Plastic tube as used for car window washers

Part V60 Pipe flange Material Brass or Aluminium 2 off

Soft Solder

Ø5
10
M3
15
2

Part V62 Stem Nut Material:- Brass or Aluminium 1 Off

M2*10PCD

2
15
5

Part V61:- Valve Wheel:- Material Brass:- 1 off

M2
4,12
5
1,5
M2
4,5
14,5
4

Part V58:- Stem Bolt Material Stainless Steel 2 off

15
2

Part V59:- Top Cover Material Brass or Aluminium:- 1 off

R5
15
Ø2.2
15

Part No V57:- Flange Material Brass or Aluminium :- 1 off

22
18
5
M5
2

Ø6
M2 Ø3
Ø11
Ø20
5
M2*10PCD

Graphite packing

Thread Loc

Part No V54:- Stop Valve Assembly

M2*5 deep 10 PCD

8,5
7
5
3
15
Ø2*10 PCD
1,5
10
13,5
20,5
2

Part No V55:- Valve Body Material Brass or Aluminium:- 1 off

M3
M2
2
5
90°
5,5
14
12,5
5
32

Part V56:- Valve Spindle Material Stainless Steel 1 off

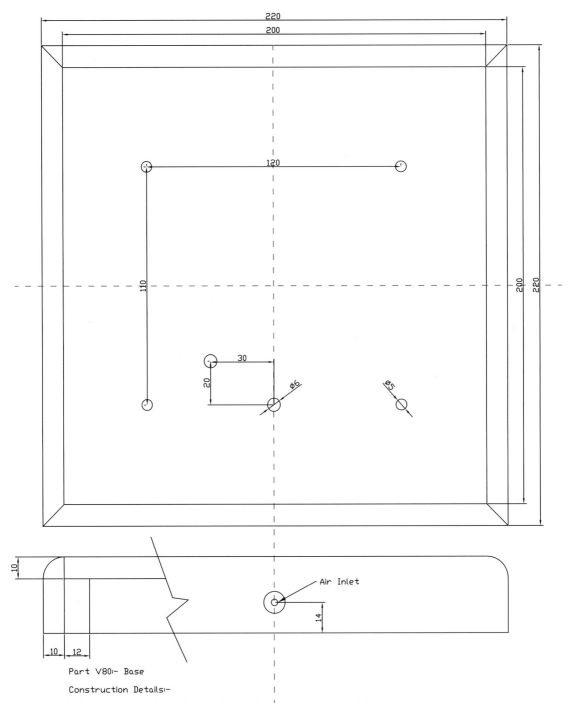

220

200

120

110

200

220

30

20

Ø6

Ø5

10

10

12

Air Inlet

14

Part V80:- Base

Construction Details:-

Material Soft wood mouldings and high density MDF:- Glue and Screw together using angle brackets.

For tile effect top, paint MDF base board with base colour, cover with masking tape. mark out tiled pattern using scalpel cut out tiles spray with contrasting colour and remove remaining masking.

slide valve on the high-pressure cylinder, this trip gear resulted in the rapid closing of the valve improving the efficiency of the engine.

The engine is fitted with a series of long bars or links that force the piston rod to move vertically up and down in the cylinder, without the use of a machined crosshead. This method of achieving parallel motion was patented by Phineas Crowther in 1800 and was applied to many colliery winding engines in the North-East coalfield. The fact that this engine still retains this feature suggests that the original engine, before its rebuild in 1900, may have been quite old. The two cylinders of 14" and 26" diameter drive two cranks set at 180 degrees with a stroke of 3ft with a central 14ft diameter flywheel, the engine drove the mill via two large leather belts running on the rim of the flywheel.

I think it's a bit fraudulent of me to claim this as a model of the Kenyon engine as I've taken huge liberties with the model in order to meet the design constraints and the objectives of the project. In fact, this is the third attempt I've made at coming up with a design for this engine, I was far from satisfied with my other attempts, my biggest problem was finding a size and scale that would do the engine justice without being too big, or with small parts that require the skill of a watchmaker.

The model is simplified by not trying to model the governor and Lumb trip gear, and replacing the slide valve with a piston valve. The part count is considerably reduced by using a single cylinder. However, for those who wish, it will be a simple matter to add a low pressure cylinder by doubling up the outside diameter of the high pressure cylinder but keeping its bore, stroke and valve arrangement the same, and then adding another crank to the end of the crank shaft.

TABLE 4: BILL OF MATERIALS FOR VERTICAL CROSS SINGLE

PART NUMBER	DESCRIPTION	QUANTITY	MATERIAL	SIZE
V3	Cylinder assembly	1		
V4	Cylinder	1	aluminium	32mm dia* 50mm 1 1/4" dia*2"
V5	Front cover	1	aluminium	35mm dia* 50mm 1 3/8" dia* 2"
V6	Rear cover	1		
V7	Cylinder base	1	aluminium	55mm dia* 15mm
V8	Valve chest	1	aluminium	16mm square*50mm 5/8" square*2"
V9	Valve rod guide	1	brass or aluminium	18mm dia* 25mm ¾" dia* 1"
V10	Valve guide stuffing box	1	brass or aluminium	10mm dia* 25mm ½" dia* 1"
V11	Piston valve	1	stainless steel or silver steel	6mm dia* 25mm ¼" dia* 1"
V12	Valve rod	1	silver steel or stainless steel	3mm dia*55mm 1/8" dia*21/4"
V13	Valve chest end closure	1	brass or aluminium	10mm dia*25mm
V14	Piston and cross head assembly	1		

(continued)

PART NUMBER	DESCRIPTION	QUANTITY	MATERIAL	SIZE
V15	Piston rod	1	brass or stainless steel	20mm dia* 25mm ¾"*1"
V16	Piston	1	brass or stainless steel	20mm dia* 25mm ¾"*1"
V17	Cross head	1	mild steel	12.7mm *12.7* 100mm ½"* ½"*4"
V18	Piston rod guide	1	brass or aluminium	10mm hex * 25mm 3/8" hex * 1"
V19	Cross head pin	1	mild steel or silver steel	6mm dia* 50mm
V20	Swing arm assembly	1		
V21	Swing arm	2	mild steel	10mm*10mm * 120mm 3/8"*3/8" * 6"
V22	Connecting rod	1	mild steel	12.7*6.7* 120mm ½" * ¼" * 5"
V23	Connecting rod bearings	2	brass or phosphor bronze	12.7 dia* 30mm ½" dia*1"
V24	Cross arm assembly	4		
V25	Cross arm rod	4	mild steel or silver steel	3mm dia* 250mm 1/8" dia* 10"
V26	Cross arm end	8	mild steel	6mm*6mm * 140mm ¼"* ¼" 6"
V27	Swing arm pin	4	silver steel	3m dia* 80mm 1/8" dia* 4"
V28	Valve rod linkage and eccentric assembly	1		
V29	Valve rod	1	silver steel	3mm dia* 130mm 1/8" dia*5"
V30	Valve rod coupling	1	mild steel	6.3mm dia* 30mm ¼" dia* 1 ½"
V31	Eccentric rod coupling	1	mild steel	6.3mm dia* 30mm ¼" dia* 1 ½"
V32	Eccentric assembly	1		
V33	Eccentric sheath	1	mild steel or brass or aluminium	32mm dia*25mm 11/4" dia*1"
V34	Eccentric inner	1	mild steel or brass	32mm dia*25mm 11/4" dia*1"

PART NUMBER	DESCRIPTION	QUANTITY	MATERIAL	SIZE
V35	Eccentric outer	1	mild Steel or brass	32mm dia*25mm 11/4" dia*1"
V36	Pillar assembly	4		
V37	Pillar	4	mild steel	10mm*10mm*700mm 3/8"*3/8"*30"
V38	Dome nut	4	brass hexagon	½" hex * 3"
V39	Rotund	8	brass or mild steel	20mm*100mm 7/8" * 4"
V40	Parallel bar	2	silver steel	4mm dia* 100mm
V41	Brass washer	4	brass	16mm dia* 40mm 5/8" * 2"
V42	Stud	4	mild steel	4mm dia* 160mm
V43	Pillar base	8	mild steel	19mm*19mm*4"
V44	Bearing stand assembly	2		
V45	Bearing stand	2	mild steel	5/16"*1 ½"*4"
V46	Main bearing	2	brass or phosphor bronze	3/8" dia*1"
V47	Crank shaft assembly	1		
V48	Crank shaft	1	mild steel or silver steel	8mm dia* 120mm
V49	Crank web	1	mild steel	8mm*30
V50	Crank pin	1	mild steel or silver steel	6mm dia* 30
V51	Valve stem guide assembly	1		
V52	Valve stem guide	1	mild steel cold rolled angle iron	¾"* ¾"* 11/4"
V53	Valve stem guide	1	mild steel cold rolled angle iron	¾"* ¾"* 11/4"
V54	Stop valve assembly	1		
V55	Valve body	1	brass	20mm dia* 40 ¾" dia* 2"
V56	Valve spindle	1	stainless steel or mild steel	5mm dia* 45mm
V57	Flange	1	brass	25mm dia* 30mm
V58	Stem bolt	1	stainless steel or mild steel	3/16" hex * 2"

(continued)

PART NUMBER	DESCRIPTION	QUANTITY	MATERIAL	SIZE
V59	Top cover	1	brass	20mm dia* 25mm ¾" dia* 1"
V60	Pipe flange	2	brass	20mm dia* 25mm ¾" dia* 1"
V61	Valve wheel	1	brass	25mm dia* 25mm 1" dia* 1"
V62	Stem nut	1	brass	20mm dia* 25mm ¾" dia* 1"
V63	Air connection assembly	1		
V64	Pipe sheath	1	thin wall brass tube	3/8" dia* 1"
V65	Feed pipe	1	thin wall brass tube	5mm dia* 40mm
V66	Spacer bush	1	brass	5mm dia* 10mm
V67	Pipe connector	1	brass	15mm dia* 20mm
V68	Top plate	1	aluminium or medium density fibreboard (MDF)	160mm * 140mm * 10mm
V69	Fabricated flywheel	1		
V70	Outer rim	1	welded mild steel tube	41/2" dia* 1 1/4" * 1/8" thick
V71	Hub	1	mild steel	1" hex * 1"
V72	Spoke	6	mild steel	6mm dia* 400mm
V73	Inner rim	1	mild steel	25mm * 400* 3mm 1" * 16" * 1/8"
V74	Alternative fabricated flywheel assembly	1		
V75	Hub washer	1	mild steel	25mm dia* 25mm 1" dia* 1"
V76	Rim	1	welded mild steel tube	100mm dia* 25mm 3mm, 5" dia*1"*1/8"
V77	Hub	1	mild steel	25mm dia* 25mm 1" dia* 1"
V78	Spoke plate	1	mild steel	100mm dia* 6.35mm 5"* ¼"
V79	Alternative cast flywheel	1	Stuart type cast flywheel	
V80	Base	1	wood and MDF	as required

CRITICAL FEATURES

Features that control alignment and symmetry are important. For instance, the cylinder front cover part V5 and piston rod guide V18 must align with the cylinder centre line. If they don't, the piston rod will bind, so it's important that the M8 thread, 4mm bore and 16mm register diameter are all concentric on the cover. Likewise, it is important that the M8 thread and 4mm bore on the piston rod guide, so these features must be machined at the same setting.

There are a number of parts with the parallel motion where symmetry is critical for ensuring a smooth action.

Swing Arm Assembly Part V20

The swing arm pins part V27 must be equal distance about the centre line of part V21 swing arm, and both arms must be a matching pair. Again, the exact distance is not that important – near enough is good enough. Armed with this understanding, the solution

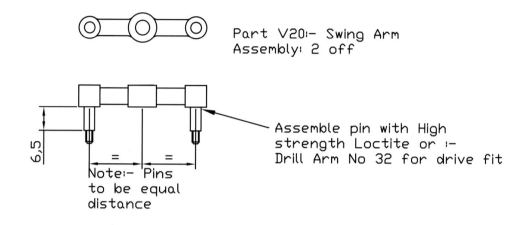

Part V20:- Swing Arm
Assembly: 2 off

Assemble pin with High
strength Loctite or :-
Drill Arm No 32 for drive fit

Note:- Pins
to be equal
distance

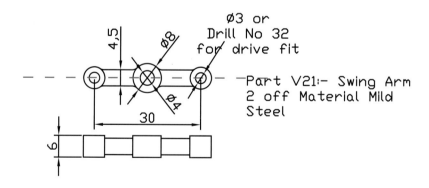

Ø3 or
Drill No 32
for drive fit

Part V21:- Swing Arm
2 off Material Mild
Steel

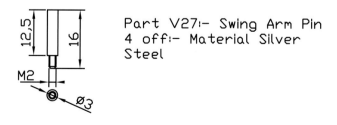

Part V27:- Swing Arm Pin
4 off:- Material Silver
Steel

Part V20 swing arm; part V21 swing arm; part V27 swing arm pin.

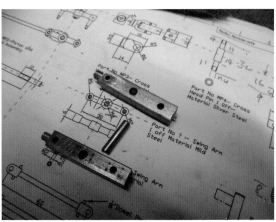

Drilling swing arms as a matched pair: note use of pin in central hole.

Drilled arms with pin.

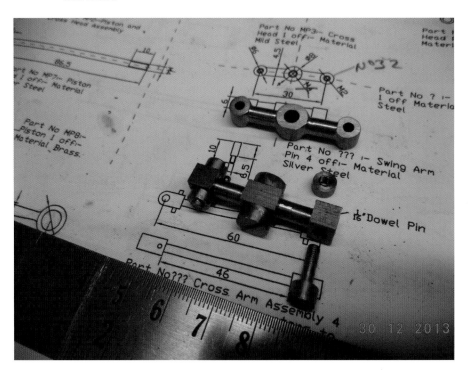

Completed swing arms.

is simple. First mark up and drill the 4mm hole in the centre of both swing arms. Then pin them together with a 4mm dowel, and then drill one 3mm hole right through both arms. Now all you have to do is rotate the arms 180 degrees on the dowel and drill the remaining 3mm holes using the first hole as a guide. The holes must end up being symmetrical and both arms must be matching.

The Cross Arms Assembly Part V24

The 60mm distance between the 3mm holes must be the same for all four assemblies. Again, a slight error in the 60mm distance won't make any difference to function, but the error must be the same in all four arms. In this case, the solution is to use a jig (Sketch V1) which can be quickly made using any suitable material you have to hand. First, cut the 3mm diameter rods to size.

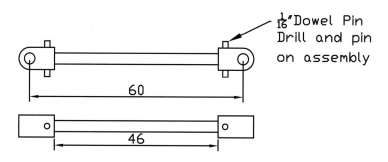

$\frac{1}{16}$" Dowel Pin
Drill and pin
on assembly

60

46

Part V24 Cross Arm Assembly 4
off:- Note 60mm hole centres to
be drilled on jig sketch ?? to
maintain repeatability centres

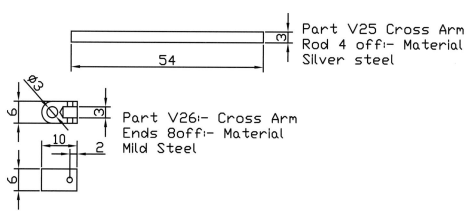

Part V25 Cross Arm
Rod 4 off:- Material
Silver steel

3

54

Ø3

6

3

6

10

2

Part V26:- Cross Arm
Ends 8off:- Material
Mild Steel

Part V24 cross arm
assembly.

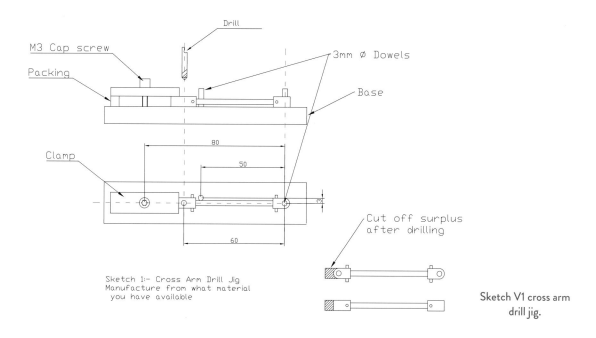

Drill

M3 Cap screw

Packing

3mm Ø Dowels

Base

Clamp

80

50

3

60

Sketch 1:- Cross Arm Drill Jig
Manufacture from what material
you have available

Cut off surplus
after drilling

Sketch V1 cross arm
drill jig.

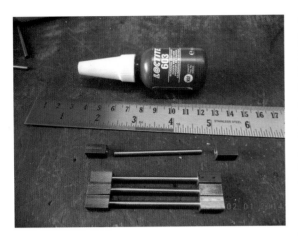

Assembled cross arms.

Try to get them all the same, then just drill the 3mm hole to take the rod in the cross arms ends. Leave them 5mm over long at this stage, fit and pin them to the rods and drill one of the 3mm cross holes in each arm. Then, using the jig, locate the drilled hole on the dowel pin. With the jig firmly clamped down, drill the other hole at the 60mm centre keeping the jig firmly clamped down. All you have to do is to drill the rest of the arms at the same setting and finish off to shape with filing buttons. As a sanity, check that they are all the same by lining them up together and passing two lengths of 3mm silver steel through the holes.

Top Plate Part V68

The engine's top plate is made from a piece 10mm thick aluminium plate, purchased from the internet. If you are lucky, you may find a piece more or less the exact size, but if your luck is as good as mine you will end up with a bit that requires cutting to size. I have a confession: I used my milling machine to get mine to size but failing this you will have to resort to the good old hack saw and a bit of hard work. If you wish, you could cheat by using MDF instead of aluminium it will certainly make things easier. One of the punishments for messing about in the training shop, when I was a first-year apprentice, was to cut a 3" length from

Cross arms on drill on jig to ensure a perfect set.

Check on alignment by passing two rods through the holes.

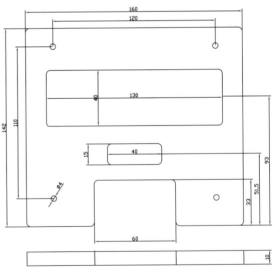

Part V68 i-Top Plate 1 off
Material 10mm thick aluminium plate

Part V68 top plate.

Chain drilling out top plate.

Filing off the dragon's teeth.

Cutting out with hack saw.

some old 2" diameter line shafting with a hacksaw. If you broke a blade, you had to cut another length off. The 3" lengths were used to make levelling jacks

that were part of the first-year tool kit we all had to make: happy days. If you struggle to keep the saw going straight, it will help if you clamp a straight edge against the plate. For the straight edge, use something that won't cause you to cry if you accidentally saw into it.

The cut outs in the top plate are done by chain drilling. You simply drill a line of 6mm holes at 7mm pitch. This is made considerably easier if you clamp a guide rail at the correct position on the drill table. Slide the part along to drill each hole at the correct pitch. This reduces the opportunity for errors to creep in. Use a hacksaw to cut through the web, and file off the dragon's teeth to give a nice neat cut out.

The Cylinder Assembly Part V3

This is exactly the same as the horizontal mill engine, except that I've increased the length by 8mm so that the engine's stroke can be increased to 40mm. The

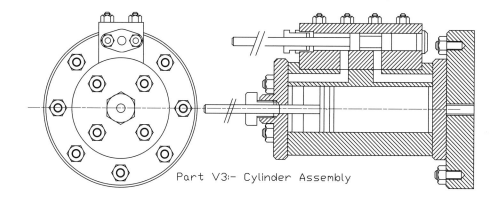

Part V3:- Cylinder Assembly

Part V3 cylinder assembly.

objective of this is to reduce the speed of the engine as I think this type of engine is best run as slow as possible so that the action of the parallel motion can be observed.

The piston and cross head assembly, and the valve rod linkage and eccentric assembly, are also similar to the horizontal mill engine parts, so what have we left are:

Cylinder Base Plate Part V7

This fastens onto the cylinder with four M3 countersunk cap screws that pass right through the rear cover part V6. Clamp the lot together with an M4 bolt with a large washer screw into the base plate to fasten the cylinder assembly to the wooden base. The base plate is made from a piece of 60mm diameter aluminium

that I got from an internet auction house. Handling something this diameter is possibly a little daunting for a beginner, but by using the correct technique it shouldn't pose too much difficulty. To grip a piece of bar this size you have to use the reverse chuck jaws. For a self-centring chuck, the jaws and the slots in the chuck body are numbered so make sure you put the right jaw in the right slot.

Face up and turn the diameter. Mark out the hole positions using the digital protractor trick, keeping the part in the chuck. Remove the chuck and move it to the drill table to drill and tap the holes on the correct PCD. Return the chuck to the lathe drill and tap the M4 centre hole, and then part off allowing 1mm for cleaning up. You may find it helps when parting off to support the work with a running centre, and don't try to go through in one go. Go part way, then move the parting

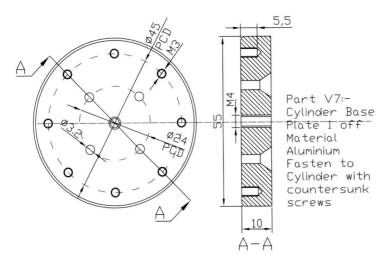

Part V7:-
Cylinder Base
Plate 1 off
Material
Aluminium
Fasten to
Cylinder with
countersunk
screws

Part V7 cylinder base plate.

Turning up the base.

Drilling and tapping the base.

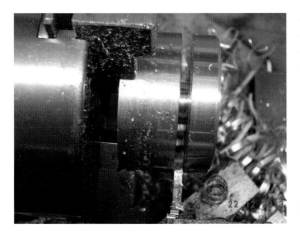

tool over 2mm and go to where you stopped. Move the tool to the middle of the slot and now go through to completely part off. This way you leave space for the chips to clear and reduce the rubbing area on the part off blade. A squirt of WD40 will help the process. Now all you have to do is to face off the reverse side and countersink the four holes for the screws.

Part V36 Pillar Assembly
Part V37 Pillar

There are four required and they are made from 3/8" square mild steel bar. First, cut them off slightly over long. In a self-centring four-jaw, carefully face them off to a length of 156mm. Try and get them all the

Parting off in steps makes the process easy.

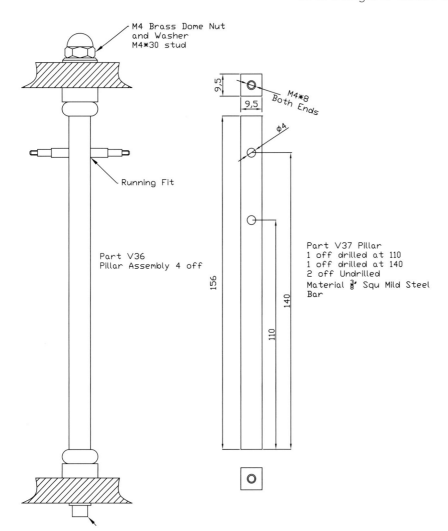

M4 Brass Dome Nut
and Washer
M4*30 stud

Running Fit

Part V36
Pillar Assembly 4 off

156

9,5

9,5

M4*8
Both Ends

Ø4

Part V37 Pillar
1 off drilled at 110
1 off drilled at 140
2 off Undrilled
Material ⅜' Squ Mild Steel
Bar

140

110

Part V36 pillar assembly
part V37 pillar.

same but it won't matter if you make them a couple of mm under this, so you will have more than one bite at the cherry. Then drill and tap both ends M4. Drill one pillar through 4mm diameter at 110mm from the end, and drill another 4mm diameter at140mm from the end to take the parallel bar part V40.

Part V38 Dome Nut

Using the radius that wears on the edge of the off-hand grinding wheel, make a form tool, then face drill and tap M4 and use the form tool to form the dome and part it off the bar. Tidy the burr up that was made at parting off.

Forming dome nut. Note use of running centre to support work.

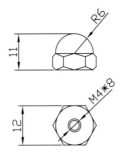

Part V38:- Dome Nut 4 off
Material ½"Brass Hexagon

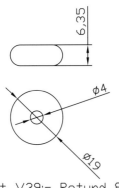

Part V39:- Rotund 8 off Material ¼"*¾" Mild Steel Bar

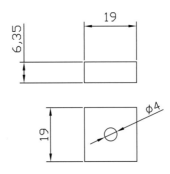

Part V43:- Pillar Base 8 off Material ¼"*¾" Mild Steel Bar

Part V38 dome nut; part V38 rotund; part V43 pillar base.

Part V39 Rotund and Part V43 Pillar Base

Made from ¼" x ¾" mild steel bar, make both parts from the same length of bar to reduce variation in the

Drill base.

Turn rotund on a mandrel.

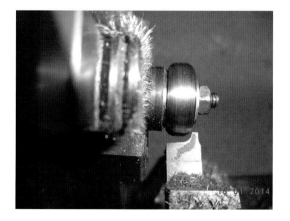

Form rotund using the same tool as used for the dome nut.

Finished base and rotund.

thickness of the final assembly. First, cut the bar into lengths and drill a 4mm hole in all their centres. The base can be filed square, but with the rotund you have make a mandrel a nice fit on the 4mm diameter hole. Mount each part to the mandrel and turn to 19mm diameter. It won't matter if you go undersize and use the same form tool used on the rotund to form the radius on one side of the rotund. Flip it round and form the radius on the other side.

Part V40 Parallel Bar

This is made from silver steel. Simply cut of a length of bar face off to length. Turn the 3mm diameter to length, and turn and thread M2 to length swap it round. Do the same for the other end.

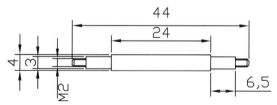

Part No V40:- Parallel Bar Shaft 2 off: Material 4mm Ø Silver Steel

Part V40 parallel bar.

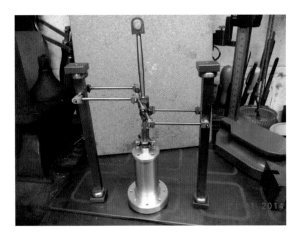

Trial assembly of parts.

Parts V41 Brass Washer and Part V42 Stud

These are simple enough parts and don't require any explanation.

Part V44 Bearing Stand Assembly

The bearing stand assembly is basically the same as for the horizontal engine except for being a little shorter, so it can quite easily be cut to shape with a hacksaw and cleaned up with a file. The most important feature is drilling the 16mm centre height for the 14mm diameter hole the same for both stands. The best way to do this is to square up the base and mark out the centre height. With the base up against the fixed jaw of the drill vice, locate the hole position

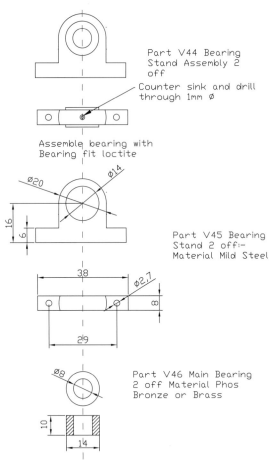

Part V44 Bearing Stand Assembly 2 off

Counter sink and drill through 1mm Ø

Assemble bearing with Bearing fit loctite

Part V45 Bearing Stand 2 off:- Material Mild Steel

Part V46 Main Bearing 2 off Material Phos Bronze or Brass

Part V44 bearing stand assembly.

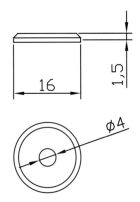

Part V4140:- Brass Washer 4 Off

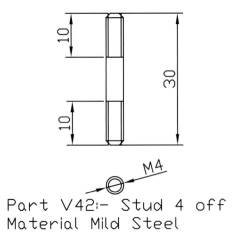

Part V42:- Stud 4 off Material Mild Steel

Part V42 stud part V41 brass washer.

firmly clamp the vice to the table and drill the first stand. Then, without moving the vice, locate the second stand and drill it at the same setting. They should all be very near to the same, and the rest is easy.

Part V47 Crank Shaft Assembly

In order to assemble the flywheel and the bearing stand, you need to be able to disassemble the crank web part V49 from the crank shaft part V48, so the web is fixed to the shaft with a M3 grub screw. To give the grub screw something to bite into, a shallow 2mm hole is drilled into the shaft. The crank pin part V50 gets the belt a braces treatment to fix it to the web using high strength Loctite plus; it is drilled and pinned. All the parts are again simple enough parts and shouldn't pose to much difficulty.

Part V51, V52 and V53 Valve Stem Guide Assembly

This is fabricated from 2" cold drawn bright mild steel angle iron. Don't use hot rolled black mild steel angle

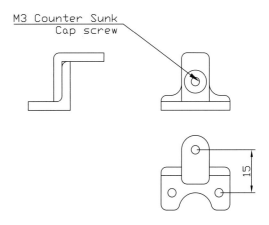

Part V51:- Valve Stem Guide Assembly 1 off

Part V51 valve stem guide assembly.

iron as its inside face will be angled and will prevent the two parts of the fabrication sitting together. Start by marking the bar out and drilling tapping and chamfering all the holes where required. Then cut it off the

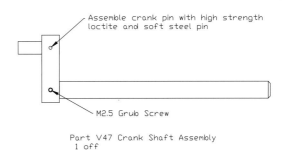

Part V47 Crank Shaft Assembly 1 off

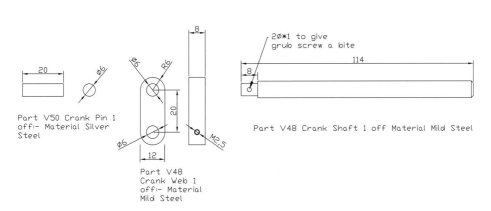

Part V47 crank shaft assembly.

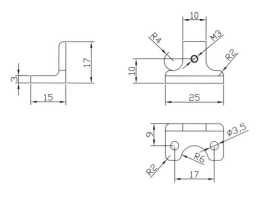

Part V52:- Valve Stem Guide Base
1 off:- Material 2" cold rolled angle iron

Part V52 valve stem guide base.

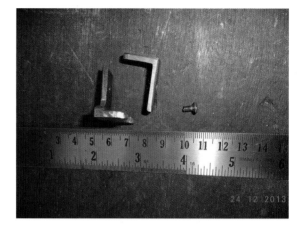

Valve stem guide parts.

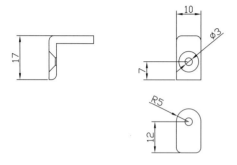

Part V53:- Valve Stem Guide Top
1 off:- Material 2" cold rolled angle iron

Part V53 valve stem guide top.

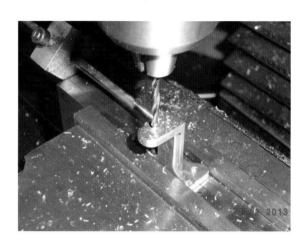

Valve stem guides assembled for final drilling.

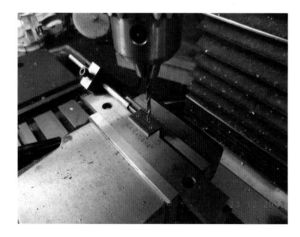

Drilling valve stem guide.

Parts assembled to cylinder.

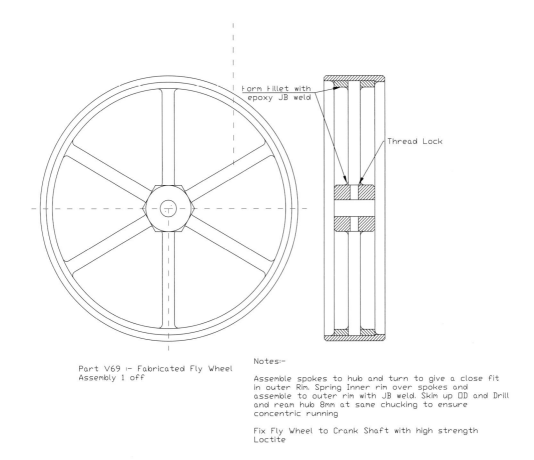

Form fillet with
epoxy JB weld

Thread Lock

Part V69 :- Fabricated Fly Wheel
Assembly 1 off

Notes:-

Assemble spokes to hub and turn to give a close fit
in outer Rim. Spring Inner rim over spokes and
assemble to outer rim with JB weld. Skim up OD and Drill
and ream hub 8mm at same chucking to ensure
concentric running

Fix Fly Wheel to Crank Shaft with high strength
Loctite

Part V69 fabricated flywheel.

bar with a hacksaw and file to shape. The two parts are held together with a M3 countersunk screws.

Part 69 Fabricated Flywheel

I enjoy experimenting with different ways of fabricating flywheels: this is a six-spoke flywheel and is fabricated from an outer rim, inner rim, spokes and hub and is all held together with the natural spring in the parts, and the epoxy resin JB weld. For those of you who don't want to try this you can use a 4" diameter Stuart flywheel or fabricate one the same as that use on the horizontal mill engine

Part 68 Outer Rim

Made from 4 ½" x 1/8" thick welded mild steel tube, you can buy short off cuts from the internet. Cut a piece off about 35mm wide to give you plenty to

clean up. Reverse the jaws on the three-jaw and clock the diameter up to run true as you can. Welded tube is far from round so get it so that it looks good to the

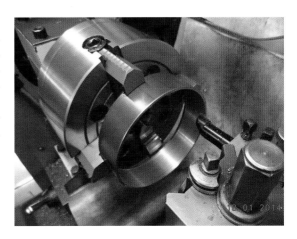

Boring outer flywheel rim.

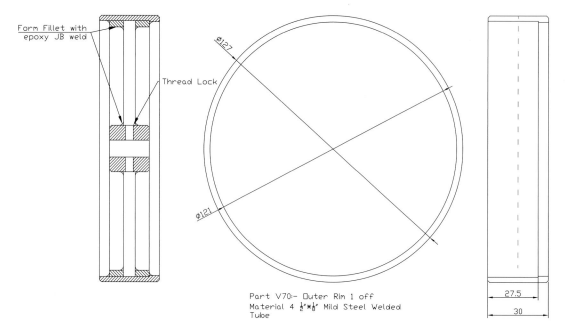

Form Fillet with epoxy JB weld

Thread Lock

Ø127

Ø121

Part V70:- Outer Rim 1 off
Material 4 ½"*⅛" Mild Steel Welded
Tube

27.5

30

Part **V70** outer rim.

eye. Face the end up, then with a boring bar clean up the internal diameter. It doesn't have to be perfectly clean, just so that the majority cleans up, leaving a step for the inner rim to butt up to. Swap it round in the chuck and face the other end up to size.

Part V73 Inner Rim

Made from a length of 1" x 1/8" thick mild steel bar. Before cutting it off to length you need to do a simple calculation, carefully measure the inside diameter of the outer rim and use it to calculate the circumference

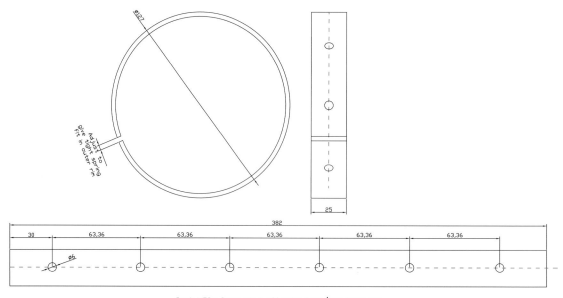

Ø127

Adjust to give tight spring Fit in outer rim

25

382

30   63,36   63,36   63,36   63,36   63,36

Ø6

Part V73:- Inner rim 1 off make from ⅛"*1" Black Mild
Steel Strip Rolled into a hoop,

Part **V73** inner rim.

Outer and inner rim.

Trial Assembly of outer and inner rim.

Slip rolls.

and drill 6 x 6 mm holes spaced along its length at this distance.

My model engineer club have a set of slip rolls available for members to use, so for me rolling the rim into a circle was easy. I had to make slight adjustment to its length in order to obtain a tight spring fit into the outer rim.

Part V71 Hub

I made this from a piece of 1" diameter mild steel bar, to help holding things together at the final machining of the assembly cut off a length 1" longer than required. Here again I cheated here somewhat in that I used my spin indexer to drill and tap M4 for the spokes. For those of you who don't have this luxury, using 1" hexagon bar will simplify things considerably. All you will have to do is index the bar round on the flats to drill and tap the holes on position.

of the midpoint of the Inner Rim Pie(D-1/8) which is the length to make the inner ring. Once you've cut it to length you need to divide the circumference by six

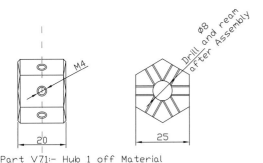

Part V71:- Hub 1 off Material $\frac{7}{8}$" Mild Steel Hexigon

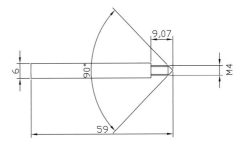

Part V72:- Spoke 6 off Material Mild Steel

Part V71 hub, part V72 spoke.

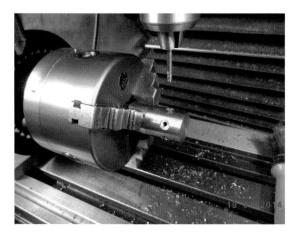

Drill and tap hub using spin indexer.

Parts ready for assembly.

Part V72 Spokes

Made from some 6mm or ¼" bar, simply cut them off 2mm longer than required turn and thread the end M4. The 60 degree cone is so that the end of the bars will nestle together when screwed in.

Assembling the Flywheel

First, assemble all the spokes in the hub with thread lock, and don't forget to give it time to go off. Mount it in the lathe and with a sharp tool gently nibble the spokes down until they are a nice close fit in the inner rim. Spring the inner ring over the spokes, apply a smear of JB weld to the mating surfaces and then with a bit of gentle persuasion with a hammer assemble it to the outer rim. Add more JB weld to form fillets, gripping on the hub chuck up in the lathe then,

Assemble with JB weld two part epoxy resin.

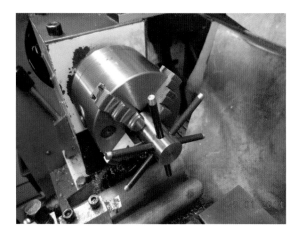

Skim down spoke in lathe.

Using nudgier to align parts for turning true.

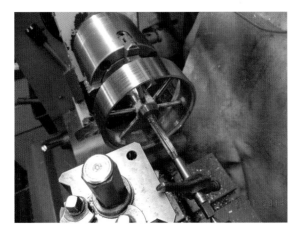

Finish turn drill and ream.

Completed flywheel.

using a nudger, persuade the outer rim to run true as you can. A nudger is simply a 1" diameter ball bearing race mounted on a holder that is used to gently apply pressure on the rim and to correct any run out. Set the assembly aside to allow the adhesive to cure.

With the adhesive fully cured and gripping on the hub, clock the rim as true as you can get it, gently face the rim and skim off the diameter again. As you are using welded tube it will be far from round so just take enough off so that the majority is cleaned off.

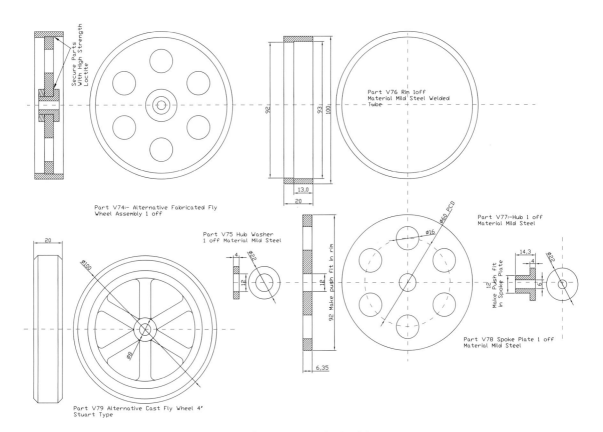

Sheet 13 of 14 alternative flywheel designs.

Then, turn the hub down to true it up and put a nice chamfer on the end, centre drill and drill and ream 8mm. Remove from the chuck and with a hacksaw remove the extra length of material you left on the hub, return to the lathe gripping on the hub just turned up, face off the cut face and skim the diameter and chamfer to match the other side, skim the rim off, if required.

For those who don't fancy using this flywheel you can use one of the alternatives as described for the horizontal mill engine.

Parts V28, V30, V31, V33, V32, V34, V35 are exactly the same as for the horizontal engine and a lot of the techniques have also been covered for this engine.

Before going on and finishing the engine off, it's now time to put it together for a trial run. You'll need to make a temporary base, any old bit of suitable chipboard will do, and a temporary air feed. Slowly and methodically assemble the parts chasing out any tight spots what you want is an engine that will turn over easily by hand. To set the valve events, a slightly different technique to the one used on the simple mill engine is require. This time we will use the exhaust ports. First, centralise the valve movement watching the piston valve through the ports, what you are looking for is the valve not quite closing the port at the limits of its travel. Make adjustments by altering the position of the coupling this is best done with the valve stem guide removed. When you've equalised the movement, set the crank at top dead centre, now undo the eccentric grub screw and rotate the eccentric so that it is at the 3 o'clock position. The eccentric follows the crank by 90 degrees. Give it a blast of air and away it should go. Let it run in with plenty of oil, when it should be happy to tick over with 10-15 psi. Now that you have it running, and you've got a big smile on your face, you can crack on and give it the finishing touches.

Part V54 Stop Valve Assembly

I thought the addition of a stop valve would neaten up the air supply arrangement. I've used this design of valve on a number of my models. I usually silver solder the parts together but, in this case, I've done away with the silver soldering and relied on fixing the flange part 58 to the body part 57 with a M5 thread and Loctite thread lock. This means you can choose to make it from aluminium or steel if you wish. I've dealt with most of the techniques

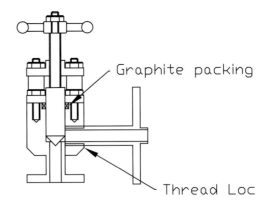

Part No V54:-
Stop Valve Assembly

Part V54 stop valve assembly.

required earlier, but a couple of parts need a little more explanation.

The Valve Body Part V54, the Top Cover Part V59 and the Stem Nut Part V62

These parts can be all made off the same length of bar. First clean up the bar and drill the tapping drill size for the 4 x M2 holes in the body. Drill the holes deep enough including allowance for the parting off blade to make all three parts. Follow this up with a 2mm drill but stop the drill short so that you can still tap the body M2. Next, finish off the stem nut by drilling and tapping a short length M3 and turning the

Valve marked out for drilling.

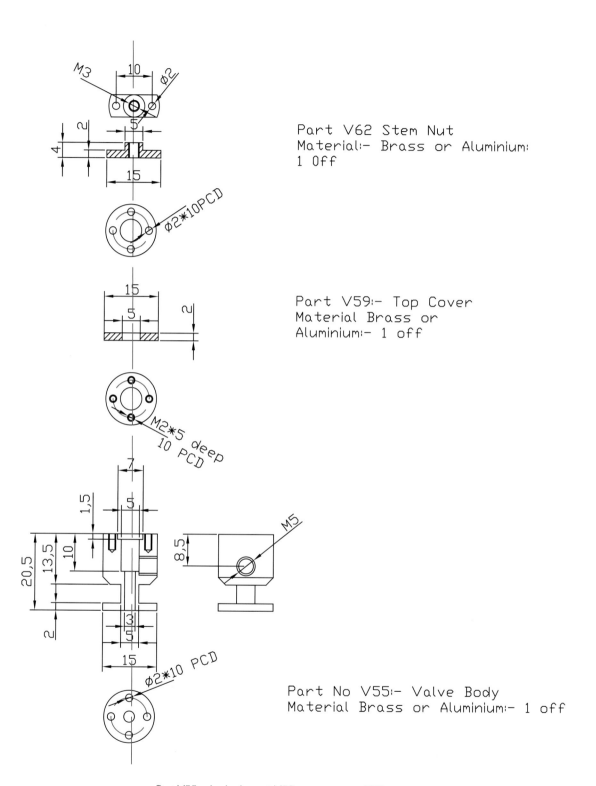

Part V62 Stem Nut
Material:- Brass or Aluminium:
1 Off

Part V59:- Top Cover
Material Brass or
Aluminium:- 1 off

Part No V55:- Valve Body
Material Brass or Aluminium:- 1 off

Part V55 valve body, part V59 top cover, part V62 stem nut.

5mm boss, part off and cut away the unwanted 2mm holes and tidy up with a file. Then drill 5mm and part off the top cover, finish off the 5mm hole to depth for the body using an 5mm slot drill or a flat bottom drill. Use the parting off tool to form the wasted portion and chamfer, part off, all that remains is to tap the four M2 holes using a tapping stand and to drill the 4 x 2mm holes in the base, and the M5 hole on the centre line for the flange. Use the rule and point method for finding the centre.

Valve Wheel Part V61

The valve wheel is made from brass. Form the wheel to shape, drill and tap M2. Mark out and drilling the four holes and return it to the chuck for parting off.

Drilling valve wheel.

Valve Spindle Part V56

This can be a tricky little beast particularly if you try to make it in one setting as you will have to turn a relatively long slender part which will flex, but again by looking at the function of each feature you can make thing simpler. The only features that have to be concentric for the valve to work correctly are the 5mm diameter and the 90 degree cone. The M3 thread as long as you make it a slack fit, doesn't need

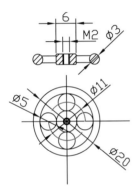

Part V61:- Valve Wheel:- Material Brass:- 1 off

Part V61 valve wheel.

Forming the valve wheel.

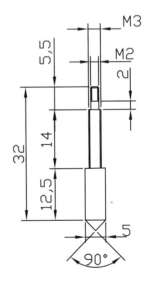

Part V56:- Valve Spindle Material Stainless Steel 1 off

Part V56 valve spindle.

Valve spindle turned in steps and coned until it falls off the bar.

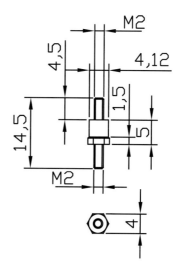

to be perfectly concentric, and the worse that can happen with the M2 thread is that the valve wheel won't run true and who will notice that. So, the solution is to turn the part in steps. Make it from 5mm diameter stainless steel or silver steel, first pull out a short length and turn and thread M2 for the 3.5mm length. Then pull out another short length and turn and thread the 14mm length of M3 thread, pull out another length and this time with the compound set at 45 degrees, towards the head stock. Turn the cone and keep going until the part falls off the bar.

Stem Bolt Part V58

This can be a tricky little beast to make because both ends of the part require threading M2. I made mine

Part V58:- Stem Bolt Material Stainless Steel 2 off

Part V58 stem bolt.

from hexagon bar, but it can be made from plain round bar which will make the threading easier.

Flange Part V57

This is a straightforward part to turn, but don't jump in and drill the 2.2mm holes until you've screwed it tight into the body. Marking the centre line for the

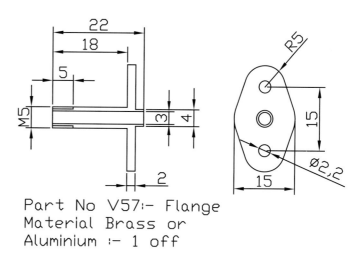

Part V57 flange.

Part No V57:- Flange Material Brass or Aluminium :- 1 off

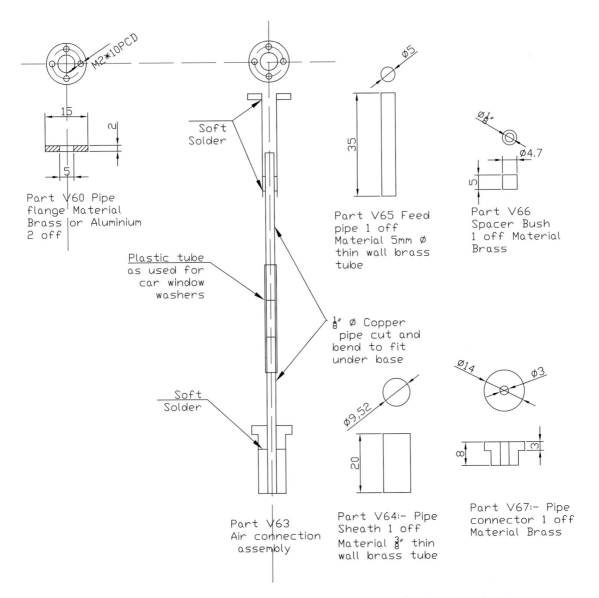

M2*10PCD

15

2

5

Part V60 Pipe
flange Material
Brass or Aluminium
2 off

Soft
Solder

Plastic tube
as used for
car window
washers

Soft
Solder

Part V63
Air connection
assembly

Ø5

35

Part V65 Feed
pipe 1 off
Material 5mm Ø
thin wall brass
tube

$\frac{1}{8}''$ Ø Copper
pipe cut and
bend to fit
under base

Ø9.52

20

Part V64:- Pipe
Sheath 1 off
Material $\frac{3}{8}''$ thin
wall brass tube

Ø$\frac{1}{8}''$

Ø4.7

5

Part V66
Spacer Bush
1 off Material
Brass

Ø14

Ø3

8

3

Part V67:- Pipe
connector 1 off
Material Brass

Part V63 air connection assembly, part V60 pipe flange, part V64 pipe sheath, part V65 feed pipe,
part V66 spacer bush, V67 pipe connector.

hole position to put them in the correct orientation, you can now drill the holes and file it to shape.

Air Connection Assembly Part V63

The parts for this are straightforward to make and are soft soldered together. The thin wall brass tube is readily available from any model making shop.

The plastic tube is the sort of stuff used on aquarium pumps or car windscreen washers, the 1/8" copper tube is available from most of the suppliers to the model engineering community. The 3/8" thin wall pipe sheath and connector simply pushes through the side of the wooden base held in place with some adhesive, bend the copper pipe to fit inside the base.

Air connection parts.

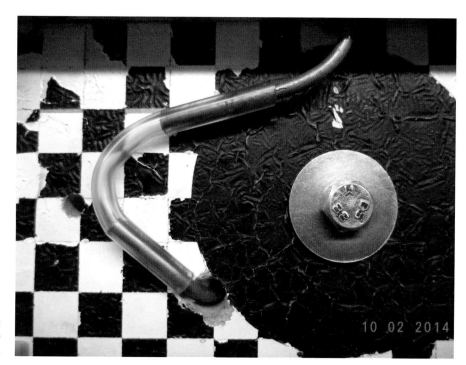

Connection made with plastic tube. Note failed attempt at tiling.

Base part V80

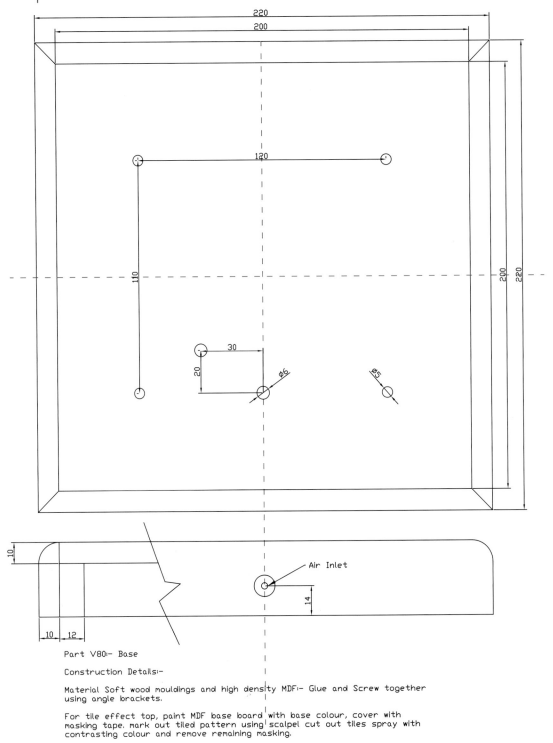

Part V80:- Base

Construction Details:-

Material Soft wood mouldings and high density MDF:- Glue and Screw together using angle brackets.

For tile effect top, paint MDF base board with base colour, cover with masking tape, mark out tiled pattern using scalpel cut out tiles spray with contrasting colour and remove remaining masking.

Part V80 base sheet 14 of 14.

The base is a fabrication: of high density MDF for the top, the surround is bull nosed soft wood with mitred corners, and an internal soft wood frame with internal plastic corner brackets. The whole lot being held together with glue and screws, stained and varnished: when it comes to woodwork, I'm no Mr Chippendale, so my attempt is far from perfect. However, the whole engine is enhanced by the tile effect base, it really sets the engine off, and I must thank 'J' for showing how to do this on the model engineering forum. I started off by first sealing the MDF with a diluted wash of PVA adhesive, when this had completely dried I sprayed a white base coat, let this completely dry, and then cover the whole lot with Frog Masking Tape it's the stuff professional decorators use so the paint doesn't creep under the edges. All you now have to

do is mark and cut out the pattern with a scalpel, and spray with a contrasting colour, then remove the rest of the masking tape. My first attempt was a disaster I just used two spray cans that I had available they were from different suppliers the topcoat melted the bottom coat and I ended up with a right mess. Yes, I know it says on the tin to do a test, but real men don't read instructions they just live with the consequence. My second attempt with two new tins from the same manufacturer on the reverse side was much better.

The cylinder cladding was done using coffee stick stirrers, stuck onto a piece of cotton cloth with Copy-dex adhesive, as for the horizontal mill engine.

That completes my second engine in my trilogy of simple engines, a process that I equally enjoyed. I'm very well pleased how the model turned out. I would

Fabricated wooden base.

Method of producing tile effect using masking tape.

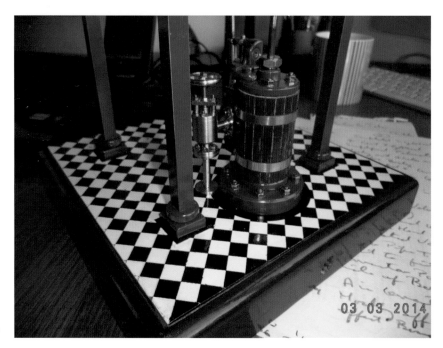

Tile effect base.

have liked to have built a more detailed model of the Kenion engine that would have done justice to the Lumb valve gear trip, but that would have required building to a far larger scale than I like to work in. Nevertheless, I hope I've captured some of the essence of the engine.

Soldering

THE GRASSHOPPER ENGINE – THE final engine in the trilogy – gives the builder the opportunity of trying their hand at fabricating parts using soft- and silver-soldering techniques, though staying true to my original objective I've included simpler alternative designs. But soldered, fabricated parts do open up a great number of opportunities for the modeller to enhance their engines by adding a great deal of interesting detail, so it's a skill well worth developing.

Soldering is the joining of metals using another filler metal of lower melting point than the parent metals. There are basically two different types of solder used by model engineers – soft solder and silver solder, sometimes called hard solder.

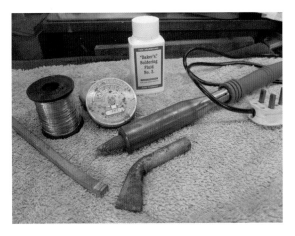

Soft soldering materials and equipment.

SOFT SOLDER

Soft soldering is used in model engineering for joints that are not normally subject to high loading such as decorative features, or for the fabrication of unpressurized water tanks. It is generally used for joining non-ferrous metal such as copper or brass, but it can also be used for joining ferrous parts.

Soft solder is nominally a tin/lead alloy, but its extensive use in the electronics industry for circuit boards, etc., has resulted in some very sophisticated soft solder grades. However, the model engineer will only need general purpose grades which are readily available from all the main suppliers to the hobby. With recent changes to the health and safety regulations, lead-free grades are replacing the leaded grades.

The joint must be free of grease and thoroughly cleaned using emery cloth or wire wool and a flux applied to the joint. The purpose of the flux is to stop the formation of oxides in the joint when it is heated. Suitable fluxes are Vaseline-based fluxes or 'backers fluid'.

The joint may be heated using a heavy-duty electrical soldering iron. Small soldering irons for electrical joints won't be capable of suppling enough heat. Gas heated irons are available and in certain circumstances the parts may be heated directly by the gas torch.

After soldering, parts should be cleaned to remove the flux using emery cloth or wire wool and cold water.

SILVER SOLDERING

Silver solder gives a stronger joint than soft solder and is used on parts that are subjected to higher loading. It is used to fabricate non-ferrous and ferrous parts, and is exclusively used to construct pressurized boilers as used on model locomotives and traction engines.

Silver solder is widely used in the jewellery trade because it is an alloy of silver, copper, tin, zinc and cadmium. Due to health and safety regulations, the use of cadmium has been phased out and there are now cadmium-free grades. By manipulating the proportions of the alloying elements, a range of melting temperatures are obtained. As with soft soldering, the range of melting temperatures can be exploited by using the technique of 'step soldering', whereby complicated assemblies can be produced by first using a higher temperature solder, followed by lower temperature solders, thus avoiding the solder in the first parts of the assembly melting.

The joint should be designed to allow a small gap between the parts to be joined so that the solder can flow into the joint via capillary action. Parts should be thoroughly de-greased and cleaned using hot soapy water, scouring pads, emery cloth or wire wool and rinsed in cold water. For non-ferrous parts, a citric acid bath may be used.

Before soldering, the joint should be fluxed. The purpose of the flux is to prevent the formation of oxides as the part is heated, preventing the parts bonding. The flux must melt before the solder. Flux is available as paste or as a powder. Flux in the powdered form is mixed into a creamy paste using water and a small drop of washing up liquid. It is relatively easy for flux to be killed (or lose it properties) by dust and other contaminates, so it is best kept in a sealed jar. For most model engineering purposes, Easy Flo 2 or Tenacity 4A is recommended. Again, this is readily available from model engineering suppliers, and is generally supplied in 250g pots.

A lot of beginners struggle with silver soldering. In most cases this can be attributed to insufficient heat. For small jobs, a DIY-type plumber's gas blow torch with disposable gas propane butane mix cartridge will be sufficient. For larger jobs, a propane gas bottle with a Sievert gas torch is recommended.

A soldering hearth is easily constructed from insulating Thermalite building blocks. They are a lot cheaper than fire bricks, and are easily obtained from building suppliers. You may even be lucky and pick up some broken blocks for free. They can be easily cut to shape, using an old saw, to construct a simple hearth. In use, their surface quickly begins to glow red adding to the heat at the work.

Silver solder is available as a rod or as a paste premixed with flux. For modelling, I would recommend buying it in rod form,1.6mm diameter (1/16) in 600mm lengths. It is relatively expensive, so it pays to use it sparingly. One of the best ways to do this is to use a trick from the jewellery trade. Cut off small lengths of solder and sit them on the joint on top of the flux

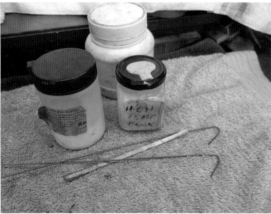

Silver solder flux and solder.

Various gas torches for silver soldering.

Homemade soldering hearth.

(jewellers call these small nuggets of solder pallions). The nuggets can be flattened with a hammer if you wish. It is best to sneak the flame up to the job: if you point the flame directly at the pallion it will simply blow off the joint. Apply the heat indirectly and soon you will see the flux beginning to change. Eventually it melts and becomes 'glassy'. At this point it is sticking the pallion in place and you can be more direct with the flame. Keep applying the flame until you see the solder beginning to melt and to flow into the joint. Try and heat the parts evenly; thicker sections should see more of the flame. Sometimes the solder will be reluctant to flow – this is usually due to the flux becoming 'tired'. Simply add more flux by dipping the hot rod into the powder, but be careful as it's easy to add more solder at this point which is wasteful.

Part prepared for silver soldering with flux and solder pallions.

TABLE 4: MELTING POINT OF COMMON SILVER SOLDERS

SOLDER	MELTING RANGE DEG C	JOINT GAP	COMMENTS
Easy Flo	608-627	0.001"	Universal general-purpose solder very free flowing contains cadmium. Lowest temperature, very small fillets
Silver Flo 55	630-660	0.001"	Cadmium-free solder nearest to Easy Flo, free flowing, produces modest fillet, good general purpose
Silver Flo 24	740-800	0.001" 0.002"	High temperature used as first step in step soldering
Silver Flo 40	650-710	0.001" 0.002"	Intermediate step in step soldering

TABLE 5: TYPES AND GRADES OF SILVER SOLDER

SOLDER	MELTING RANGE DEG C	JOINT GAP	COMMENTS
Easy Flo	608-627	0.001"	Universal general-purpose solder very free flowing contains cadmium. Lowest temperature, very small fillets
Silver Flo 55	630-660	0.001"	Cadmium-free solder nearest to Easy Flo, free flowing, produces modest fillet, good general purpose
Silver Flo 24	740-800	0.001" 0.002"	High temperature used as first step in step soldering
Silver Flo 40	650-710	0.001" 0.002"	Intermediate step in step soldering

TABLE 6: FLUXES FOR USE WITH SILVER SOLDER

FLUX	TEMP DEG C	CLEANING	COMMENTS
Easy Flo	550-800	Acid, cold or hot water	Universal general-purpose flux suitable for most M.E applications
Tenacity 4A	600-850	Acid, cold or hot water rinse	For higher temperature solders and longer activity

Clean and pickle overnight in citric acid, then wash off with cold water and fettle off any surplus solder. If you get it right, there will be no surplus to clean off. The acid pickle is best made up with citric acid. This is easily obtained in powder-form from a chemist or a home brewing supplier. You'll need about 1oz to a gallon of water in a plastic bucket. Add a few drops of bleach to prevent the formation of mold on the surface. Keep covered and the mixture will keep for three or four months.

Health and Safety

Be careful of starting a fire. Remove all combustible material clear of the soldering area. Never breathe in fumes from the process. Keep the area well ventilated. Don't get flux on your skin as it's an irritant. Let the work and hearth cool down before risking touching it, or use a pair of blacksmith's tongs to pick it up and quench in water. Also be careful not to pick the soldering rod up by the hot end. If you bend the cold end over and always pick it up by that end you will avoid burning your fingers.

Grasshopper Engine Component Manufacture 7

THE ENGINE IS ROUGHLY based on an engine displayed at the Museum of Science and Industry in Manchester, and dates from the 1850s. It was used to haul minerals up an incline at an alkaline works. It can run in reverse by using a simple slip eccentric allowing it to haul in both directions.

This engine is a little more challenging for the beginner as it uses a larger laser cut flywheel. I've fabricated some of the parts using silver solder in order to replicate some of the artistic features of the engine. A small milling machine will also be required for some parts. However, for those who prefer something simpler, I've included less-challenging options that can be produced in a more modestly equipped workshop.

I had this engine in my sights for a number of years, but I had a big problem in coming up with a suitable flywheel. I try to avoid casting wherever possible, but engines from this period tend to have quite

Completed model of Grasshopper haulage engine. Grasshopper haulage engine, open frame horizontal engine.

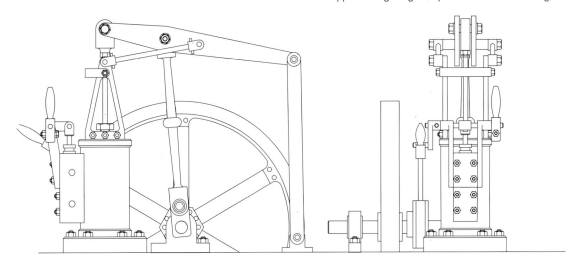

Note:- Some Parts are Not Shown to Aid Clarity
General Assembly Drawing
Part G1

Part G1 general assembly Grasshopper haulage engine.

large diameter flywheels that are of a light, fabricated construction and none of my previous methods would produce a suitable flywheel. I toyed with various ideas, but I felt they were all too complicated and outside my design constraints. Suitable castings are available from a number of different suppliers, but they are only available as part of a set, and the cost ruled out this option. I then hit upon the idea of having a blank flywheel laser cut. Laser cutting firms can be found in your local trade directory as laser cutting is widely used in industry and there is no shortage of firms willing to take on this work. You will have to provide them with a sketch of the flywheel from which they will produce their own drawing to programme their machine.

If you would prefer to use a cast flywheel, a 10" flywheel can be obtained from RDG Tools (usual disclaimer) but you will have to increase all the drawing sizes by 50 per cent.

Again, the design uses a number of parts that are common – or very similar to – parts described for the horizontal and vertical builds so I will only describe the manufacture of parts that are specific to the Grasshopper engine.

TABLE 7: BILL OF MATERIALS FOR A GRASSHOPPER HAULAGE ENGINE

PART NUMBER	DESCRIPTION	QUANTITY	MATERIAL	SIZE
G1				
G1	General assembly drawing			
G2	Cylinder assembly			
G3	Front cover	1	aluminium	35mm dia* 50mm
G4	Rear cover	1		1 3/8" dia* 2"
G5	Cylinder	1	aluminium	32mm dia* 50mm
				1 1/4" dia*2"
G6	Cylinder base	1	aluminium	
G7	Valve rod guide	1	brass or aluminium	18mm dia* 25mm
				¾" dia* 1"
G8	Valve guide stuffing box	1	brass or aluminium	10mm dia* 25mm
				½" dia* 1"
G9	Piston valve	1	stainless steel or silver steel	6mm dia* 25mm
				¼" dia* 1"
G10	Valve chest	1	aluminium	16mm square*50mm
				5/8" square*2"
G11	Valve chest end closure	1	brass or aluminium	10mm dia*25mm
G12	Valve rod	1	silver steel	3mm dia* 35mm
				1/8" dia* 13/8"
G13	Beam assembly			

PART NUMBER	DESCRIPTION	QUANTITY	MATERIAL	SIZE
G14	Beam	2	mild steel	16mm * 3mm * 280mm 5/8" * 1/8" * 12"
G15	Swivel pin	2	mild steel	6mm dia* 40mm ¼" dia* 15/8"
G16	Beam spacer	4	mild steel	5mm dia* 48mm ¼" dia* 2"
G17	Beam stub shaft	2	mild steel	5mm dia* 55mm ¼" dia* 2"
G18	Vertical beam assembly			
G19	Side arm	2	brass	9mm*3mm*260mm 3/8" * 1/8" *11"
G20	Interlocking ring	7	brass	20mm dia*70mm
G21	Alternative design of vertical beam			
G22	Alternative side arm	2	brass or mild steel	9mm*3mm*260mm 3/8" * 1/8" *11"
G23	Spacers for alternative beam	4	brass or mild steel	6mm dia* 100mm ¼" dia* 4"
G24	Swivel base	1	mild steel	15mm*20mm*20mm 5/8"*7/8"*7/8"
G25	Connecting rod	1	mild steel	12mm*6mm*120mm ½"*1/4"*5"
G26	A frame assembly			
G27	A frame	2	mild steel	26mm * 3mm*110mm 1"*1/8"* 41/2"
G28	Alternative A frame	2	mild steel	26mm * 3mm*110mm 1"*1/8"* 41/2"
G29	A frame base	1	mild steel	25mm*5mm*26mm 1"*1/4"*1"
G30	A frame brace	1	mild steel	6mm*6mm*70mm ¼"*1/4"*3"
G31	Piston assembly			
G32	Piston rod guide	1	brass	10mm hex *15mm 3/8" hex*5/8"
G33	Cross head assembly	1	mild steel	12mm*6mm*15mm ½"*1/4"*5/8"

(continued)

PART NUMBER	DESCRIPTION	QUANTITY	MATERIAL	SIZE
G34	Bearing	1	brass or phos bronze	10mm dia*15mm 3/8"dia*5/8"
G35	Piston	1	brass or phos bronze	20mm dia*25mm 7/8"*1"
G36	Piston rod	1	silver steel	4mm dia*100mm
G37	Main bearing assembly	2		
G38	Bearing stand	2	mild steel	5/16"*1 ½"*3"
G39	Main bearing	2	brass or phosphor bronze	3/8" dia*1"
G40	Cross arm assembly	2		
G41	Cross arm rod	2	silver steel	3mm dia*125mm 1/8" dia* 5"
G42	Cross arm end	4	mild steel	6mm*6mm * 140mm ¼"* ¼" 6"
G43	Crank shaft assembly	1		
G44	Crank pin	1	mild steel	6mm dia*30mm
G45	Crank web	1	mild steel	12mm*8mm*30mm ½"*3/8"8*11/4"
G46	Crank shaft	1	mild steel or silver steel	8mm dia*120mm
G47	Eccentric pin	1	mild steel or silver steel	3mm dia*20mm
G48	Eccentric assembly	1		
G49	Method of fabrication	1		
G50	Alternative eccentric assembly	1		
G51	Eccentric valve link	1	mild steel	6mm*9mm*50 ¼"*3/8"*2"
G52	Eccentric sheath	1	brass	35mm Dia*25mm 1/3/8"Dia*1"
G53	Eccentric inner	1	mild steel	
G54	Eccentric outer	1	mild steel	
G55	Valve linkage assembly	1		
G56	Handle	1	mild steel	¼"*1/4"*2"

PART NUMBER	DESCRIPTION	QUANTITY	MATERIAL	SIZE
G57	Central valve crank	1	mild steel	3/8"*3/8"*1"
G58	Valve crank arm	1	mild steel	3/8"*3/8"*1"
G59	Valve crank pin	1	mild steel	6mm dia*25mm ¼" dia*1"
G60	Valve lever bracket	1	mild steel	1"*1"*2" box section
G61	Swivel pin	1	silver steel	3mm dia*60mm 1/8" dia*21/4"
G62	Forked link	1	mild steel	9mm*9mm*40mm 3/8"*3/8"*13/4"
G63	Flywheel assembly	1		
G64	Laser cut flywheel	1	mild steel	laser cut to profile
G65	Machined flywheel	1		
G66	Outer hub	1	mild steel	1"Hex*11/2"
G67	Inner hub	1	mild steel	1"Hex*11/2"
G68	Whistle assembly	1		
G69	Valve connector	1	brass	10mm dia*40mm
G70	Valve body	1	brass	10mm dia*40mm
G71	Lever	1	mild steel	3mm*13mm*25 1/8"*1/2"*1"
G72	Body	1	thin wall brass tube	¼" dia*2"
G73	Whistle disc	1	brass	9mm*25mm
G74	Whistle connector	1	brass	5/32" Hex*1"
G75	Mounting bracket	1	brass strip	10mm*1mm*50mm
G76	Lock nut	1	brass	¼" Hex*1"
G77	Pipe connector	1	brass	3/16"*40 ME union nut and olive and 3/32"copper tube
G78	Regulator assembly	1		
G79	Top cover	1	brass or aluminium	15mm dia*25MM 5/8" dia*1"
G80	Stem bolt	1	brass	3/16" Hex *1"
G81	Spindle	1	stainless steel	5mmDia*50mm
G82	Body	1	brass or aluminium	25mm dia*50mm 1" dia*2"

(continued)

PART NUMBER	DESCRIPTION	QUANTITY	MATERIAL	SIZE
G83	Stem nut	1	brass or aluminium	25mm dia*50mm 1" dia*2"
G84	Regulator handle	1	mild steel	6mm*6mm*50mm ¼"*1/4"*2"
G85	Bedplate	1	aluminium jig plate or MDF	100mm*200mm*10mm
G86	Wooden base	1	soft wood as required	

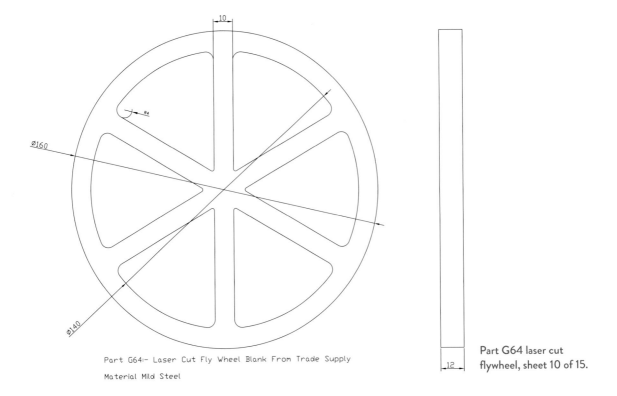

Part G64:- Laser Cut Fly Wheel Blank From Trade Supply
Material Mild Steel

Part G64 laser cut flywheel, sheet 10 of 15.

Machining the Flywheel Part G65

The laser cut blank is machined in more or less the same way as you would machine a cast flywheel. The first job is to clean away any flashing and burs. Being laser cut, there were very few, and they were soon dealt with using a Dremel fitted with a rotary burr. I have a large 6" independent four-jaw chuck, and with the jaws reversed it easily held the flywheel which was clocked up so it was running reasonably true, faced up and the recess for the spokes was machined. It was then centre drilled and the bore rough drilled. It was then reversed in the chuck, the bore clocked up, faced and the spokes thinned, and this time I bored the centre to the finished size. I then turned up a mandrel a nice close fit on the bore and bolted the flywheel to this for turning up its rim. Only being fixed at its centre meant this turning process made the flywheel hum musically, but I got a good finish, so it worked well.

Laser cut flywheel as delivered.

Pushing the Boat into Complicated Waters

Flywheels from this time were often fabricated from a number of cast parts, and bolted or riveted together, so I wanted to simulate this. The end of the spokes were marked out simply and, using the mandrel with a chuck clamped to the drill table to hold the flywheel, rotated round and drilled for 1/16" brass rivets.

Hub Assembly Parts G66, G67

I had a short length of suitable 1" Hexagon in my scrap box, but 1" round would have done the job just as well. The parts are easy enough to make, just concentrate on getting a close fit of the outer hub in the flywheel and making the inner hub a close fit in the outer. No great precision is required to drill the holes for the 1/16" rivets, just simply mark out using the lathe chuck jaws to guide the index for the marking out. Slightly countersink the back of the holes so that the rivets can be peened over and filed off smooth. Assemble the hub to the wheel using high strength Loctite.

If you don't have a large four-jaw, you could quite easily mount it on a face plate, moving the clamps around to gain access to unturned areas, if you are not too bothered about the flywheel looking quite so authentic, you could simplify the process further by not skimming the faces at all. The laser cut finish on my wheel was good enough to be left more or less as supplied with just a little bit of fettling. All that is needed is to drill the bore out so that it runs reasonably true.

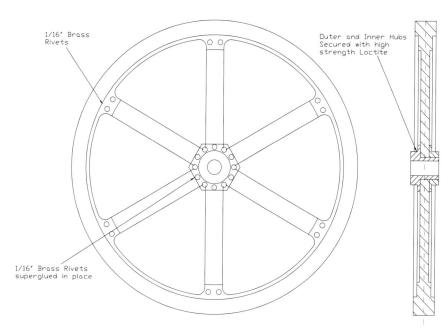

1/16' Brass Rivets

1/16' Brass Rivets superglued in place

Outer and Inner Hubs Secured with high strength Loctite

Part G63:- Fly Wheel Assembly

Part G63 flywheel assembly, sheet 9 of 15.

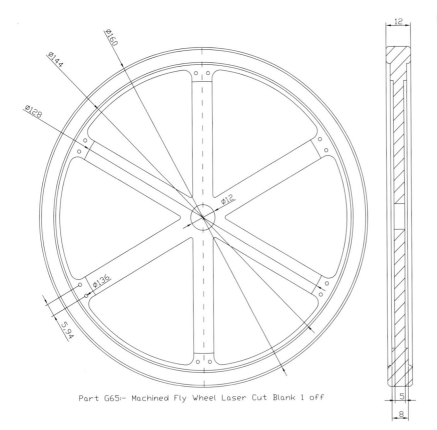

Part G65 machined flywheel.

Part G65:- Machined Fly Wheel Laser Cut Blank 1 off

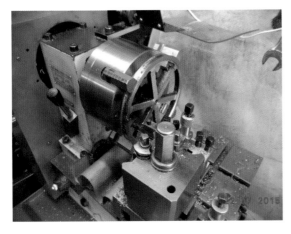

Machining flywheel in large four jaw chuck.

Boring out for hub.

Cylinder Base Part G6

Made from a slice of 45mm diameter aluminium, set up in the three-jaw chuck with the jaws reversed, face off and drill and tap M4. This will be used to clamp the cylinder to the wooden base. Flip it round in the chuck, face to length and chamfer the edge. Using the rear cover (part G4) as a template, mark off the position of the four holes, drill 3.2mm and chamfer the back edge to take countersunk screws. Mark out the position for the 8 x M3 studs and drill and tap. These are only for appearance and may be omitted if you wish.

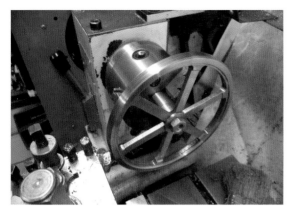

Skimming the OD with wheel mounted on a mandrel.

Drilling rim for rivets.

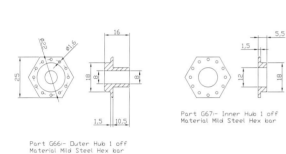

Part G66 outer hub, part G67 inner hub.

Drilling hub for rivets.

Flywheel parts for assembly.

Assembled flywheel.

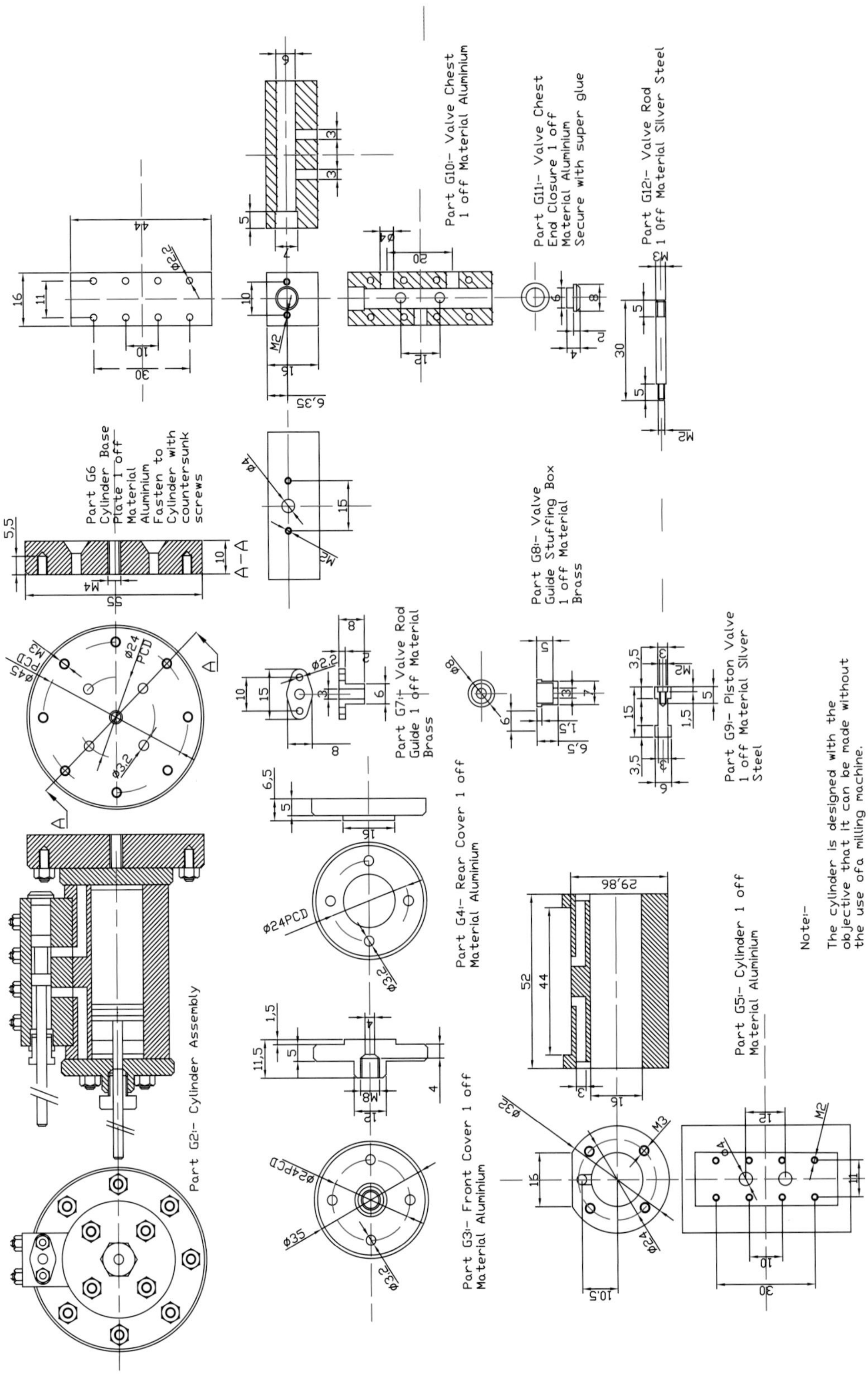

Part G2:- Cylinder Assembly

Part G6:- Cylinder Base Plate 1 off Material Aluminium Fasten to Cylinder with countersunk screws

Part G10:- Valve Chest 1 off Material Aluminium

Part G11:- Valve Chest End Closure 1 off Material Aluminium Secure with super glue

Part G12:- Valve Rod 1 off Material Silver Steel

Part G8:- Valve Guide Stuffing Box 1 off Material Brass

Part G7:- Valve Rod Guide 1 off Material Brass

Part G9:- Piston Valve 1 off Material Silver Steel

Part G4:- Rear Cover 1 off Material Aluminium

Part G3:- Front Cover 1 off Material Aluminium

Part G5:- Cylinder 1 off Material Aluminium

Note:-

The cylinder is designed with the objective that it can be made without the use of a milling machine.

Cylinder assembly, sheet 2 of 15.

Part G6 cylinder base.

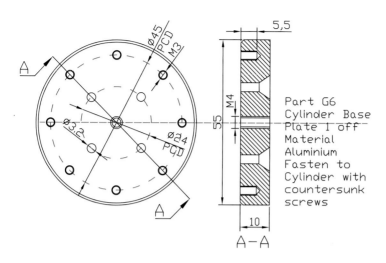

Ø45 PCD M3

Ø3.2

Ø24 PCD

5,5

M4

55

10

A—A

Part G6
Cylinder Base
Plate 1 off
Material
Aluminium
Fasten to
Cylinder with
countersunk
screws

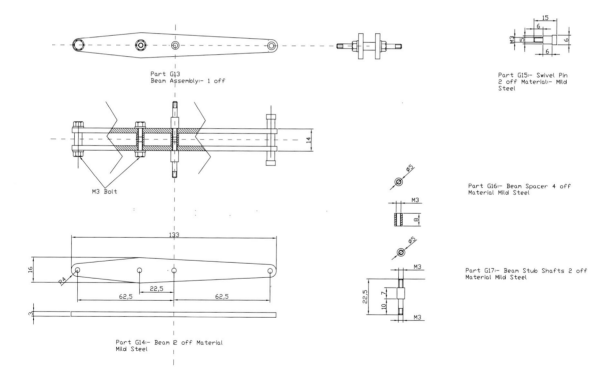

Part G13
Beam Assembly:- 1 off

15
6
M3
6
6

Part G15:- Swivel Pin
2 off Material:- Mild
Steel

14

M3 Bolt

Ø5

Part G16:- Beam Spacer 4 off
Material Mild Steel

M3

8

133

16

R4

22,5

62,5   62,5

3

Part G14:- Beam 2 off Material
Mild Steel

Ø5

M3

22,5

10 7

M3

Part G17:- Beam Stub Shafts 2 off
Material Mild Steel

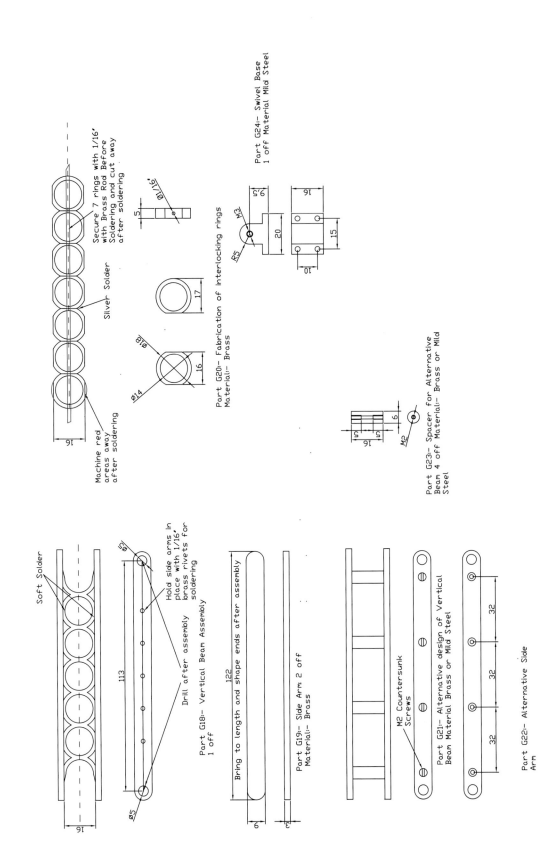

Secure 7 rings with 1/16' with Brass Rod Before Soldering and cut away after soldering

Silver Solder

Machine red areas away after soldering

16

5

Ø1/16'

17

Ø18

Ø14

16

Part G20:- Fabrication of interlocking rings
Material:- Brass

Part G24:- Swivel Base
1 off Material Mild Steel

M3

R5

20

9

5

16

15

10

Part G23:- Spacer for Alternative Beam 4 off Material:- Brass or Mild Steel

M2

6

5 5

16

Soft Solder

Hold side arms in place with 1/16' brass rivets for soldering

Ø5

Drill after assembly

113

Part G18:- Vertical Beam Assembly
1 off

16

Ø5

Bring to length and shape ends after assembly

122

Part G19:- Side Arm 2 off
Material:- Brass

6

3

M2 Countersunk Screws

Part G21:- Alternative design of Vertical Beam Material Brass or Mild Steel

32 32 32

Part G22:- Alternative Side Arm

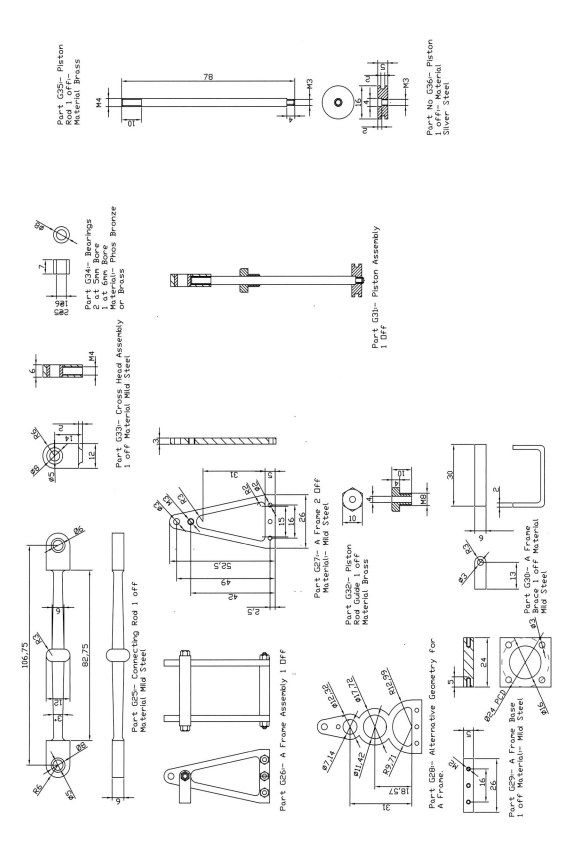

Part G35:- Piston Rod 1 off:- Material Brass

Part No G36:- Piston 1 off:- Material Silver Steel

Part G34:- Bearings 2 at 5mm Bore 1 at 6mm Bore Material:- Phos Bronze or Brass

Part G31:- Piston Assembly 1 Off

Part G33:- Cross Head Assembly 1 off Material Mild Steel

Part G25:- Connecting Rod 1 off Material Mild Steel

Part G27:- A Frame 2 Off Material:- Mild Steel

Part G32:- Piston Rod Guide 1 off Material Brass

Part G30:- A Frame Brace 1 off Material Mild Steel

Part G26:- A Frame Assembly 1 Off

Part G28:- Alternative Geometry for A Frame.

Part G29:- A Frame Base 1 off Material:- Mild Steel

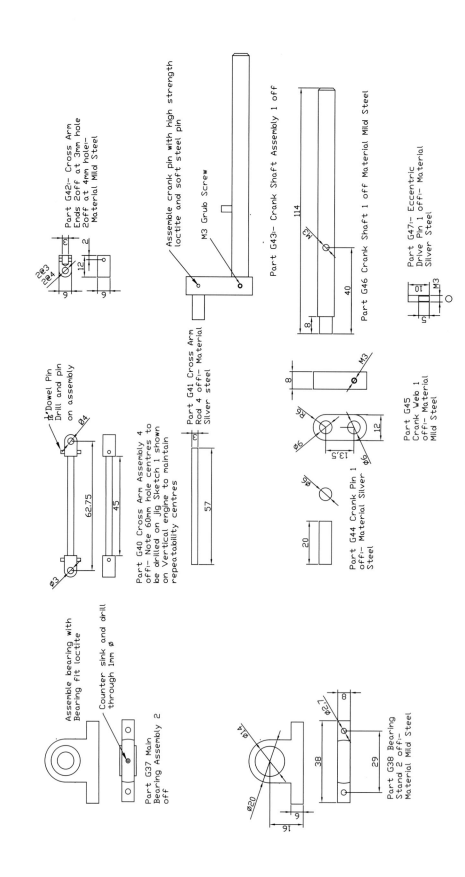

Part G42:- Cross Arm
Ends 2off at 3mm hole
2off at 4mm hole:-
Material Mild Steel

2⌀3
2⌀4

Assemble crank pin with high strength
loctite and soft steel pin

M3 Grub Screw

Part G43:- Crank Shaft Assembly 1 off

Part G46 Crank Shaft 1 off Material Mild Steel

Part G47:- Eccentric
Drive Pin 1 off:- Material
Silver Steel

Dowel Pin
Drill and pin
on assembly

⌀4

⌀3

Part G40 Cross Arm Assembly 4
off:- Note 60mm hole centres to
be drilled on Jig Sketch 1 shown
on Vertical engine to maintain
repeatability centres

Part G41 Cross Arm
Rod 4 off:- Material
Silver steel

Part G45
Crank Web 1
off:- Material
Mild Steel

Part G44 Crank Pin 1
off:- Material Silver
Steel

Assemble bearing with
Bearing fit loctite

Counter sink and drill
through 1mm ⌀

Part G37 Main
Bearing Assembly 2
off

Part G38 Bearing
Stand 2 off:-
Material Mild Steel

Part G39 Main Bearing
2 off Material Phos
Bronze or Brass

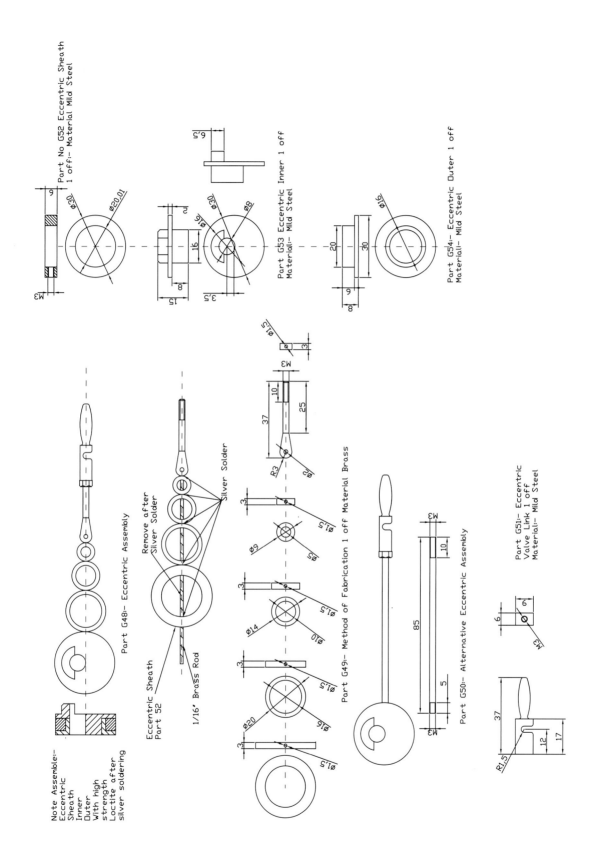

Part No G52 Eccentric Sheath 1 off:- Material Mild Steel

Part G53 Eccentric Inner 1 off
Material:- Mild Steel

Part G54:- Eccentric Outer 1 off
Material:- Mild Steel

Part G48:- Eccentric Assembly

Remove after
Silver Solder

Silver Solder

Eccentric Sheath
Part 52

1/16" Brass Rod

Part G49:- Method of Fabrication 1 off Material Brass

Part G50:- Alternative Eccentric Assembly

Part G51:- Eccentric
Valve Link 1 off
Material:- Mild Steel

Note Assemble:-
Eccentric
Sheath
Inner
Outer
With high
strength
Loctite after
silver soldering

GRASSHOPPER ENGINE COMPONENT MANUFACTURE   139

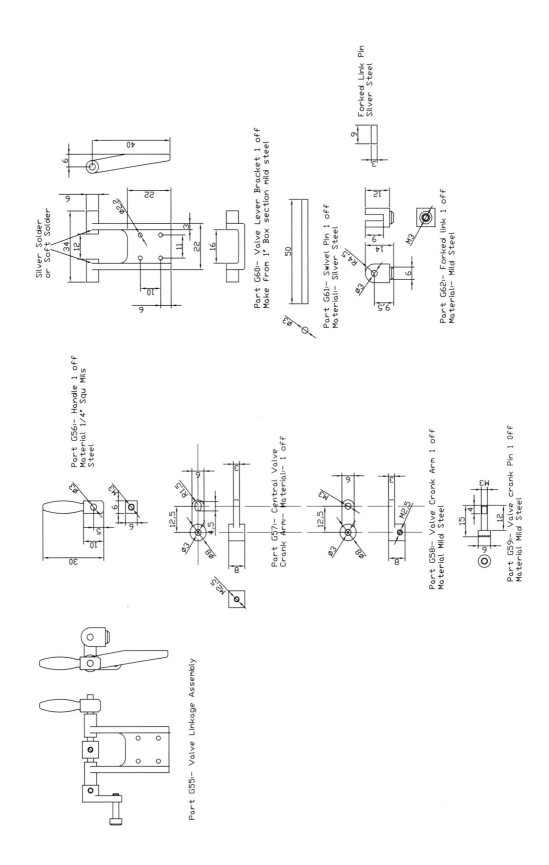

Part G56:- Handle 1 off
Material 1/4" Squ Mils
Steel

Part G60:- Valve Lever Bracket 1 off
Make from 1" Box section mild steel

Silver Solder
or Soft Solder

Forked Link Pin
Silver Steel

Part G61:- Swivel Pin 1 off
Material:- Silver Steel

Part G62:- Forked link 1 off
Material:- Mild Steel

Part G57:- Central Valve
Crank Arm:- Material:- 1 off

Part G58:- Valve Crank Arm 1 off
Material Mild Steel

Part G59:- Valve crank Pin 1 Off
Material Mild Steel

Part G55:- Valve Linkage Assembly

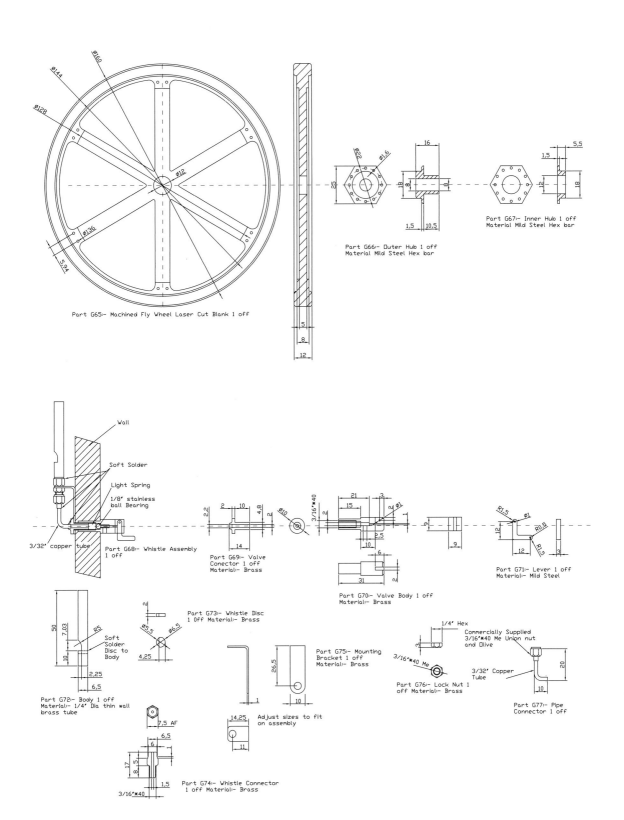

Part G65:- Machined Fly Wheel Laser Cut Blank 1 off

Part G66:- Outer Hub 1 off
Material Mild Steel Hex bar

Part G67:- Inner Hub 1 off
Material Mild Steel Hex bar

Wall

Soft Solder

Light Spring

1/8' stainless
ball Bearing

3/32' copper tube

Part G68:- Whistle Assembly
1 off

Part G69:- Valve
Conector 1 off
Material:- Brass

Part G70:- Valve Body 1 off
Material:- Brass

Part G71:- Lever 1 off
Material:- Mild Steel

Part G73:- Whistle Disc
1 Off Material:- Brass

Soft
Solder
Disc to
Body

Part G72:- Body 1 off
Material:- 1/4' Dia thin wall
brass tube

Part G75:- Mounting
Bracket 1 off
Material:- Brass

Adjust sizes to fit
on assembly

1/4' Hex

3/16'*40 Me

Commercially Supplied
3/16'*40 Me Union nut
and Olive

Part G76:- Lock Nut 1
off Material:- Brass

3/32' Copper
Tube

Part G77:- Pipe
Connector 1 off

7,5 AF

3/16'*40

Part G74:- Whistle Connector
1 off Material:- Brass

Beam Assembly Part G13

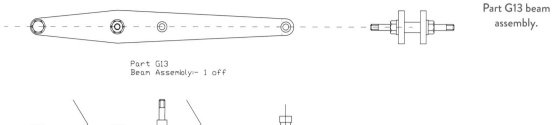

Part G13 beam assembly.

Part G13
Beam Assembly:- 1 off

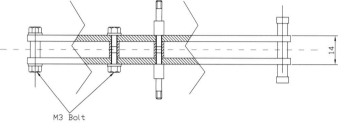

M3 Bolt

14

Beam Part G14

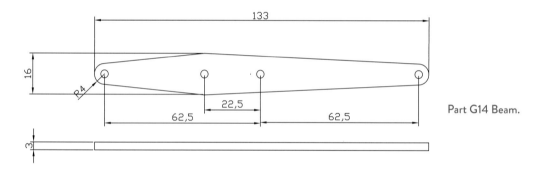

Part G14 Beam.

133

16

P4

22,5

62,5   62,5

3

Part G14:- Beam 2 off Material
Mild Steel

The beam is made from a length of 5/8" x 1/8" mild steel strip. Start by cutting the two halves of the beam to length, leaving yourself a couple of extra mm on the length for finishing, then mark the centre of each beam, and on one mark out the rest of the hole positions. Drill the centre hole in each beam and with an M3 screw bolt the two beams together. Now you can drill the rest of the holes; this way both beams will be exactly the same. Using a hacksaw and a file, nibble away the material to make the tapered beam and use filing buttons to make a nice neat job of shaping the ends.

Beam marked out.

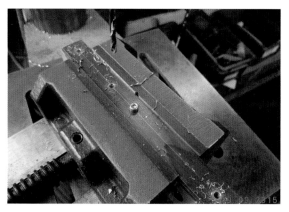

Beams drilled together to make a perfectly matching pair.

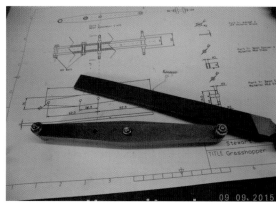

Beams filled to shape.

Swivel Pin Part G15 and Stub Shaft Part G17

These two parts are similar and are both made from ¼″ hexagon bar but you could use round bar if you wish. There's not much to them and should pose you little problem.

Beam Spacer Part G16

These can be made from mild steel or brass. The two on the left of the beam act as journals for the connecting rod and the piston cross head. The important thing here is to face all four off to the same length.

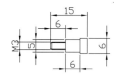

Part G15:- Swivel Pin
2 off Material:- Mild
Steel

Part G16:- Beam Spacer 4 off
Material Mild Steal

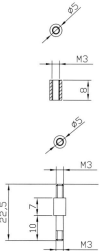

Part G17:- Beam Stub Shafts 2 off
Material Mild Steel

Part G15 swivel pin, part G16 beam spacer, part G17 beam stub shafts.

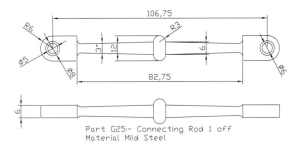

106,75

82,75

R6

R3

3°

12

6

Ø5

Ø6

Ø6

6

Part G25:- Connecting Rod 1 off
Material Mild Steel

7

Ø8

2Ø5
1Ø6

Part G34:- Bearings
2 at 5mm Bore
1 at 6mm Bore
Material:- Phos Bronze
or Brass

Connecting Rod Part G25

I used a length of ½" square mild steel for this part as it meant I could grip it in the self-centring four-jaw chuck and use my milling machine to reduce the thickness down to 6mm after I had done the turning. You could use a piece of ½" x 1/4" bar and use a four-jaw independent chuck, or use the same method as employed on the horizontal and vertical engines of centring each end of the bar and turning it between centres. Whichever method you use, the steps are very similar. Start by facing both ends of the bar off square and mark the overall distance between the bearings and its general overall shape, and use small centre pops to mark the lines so that you don't lose them.

Marking out connecting rod.

Using parting tool to rough out shape.

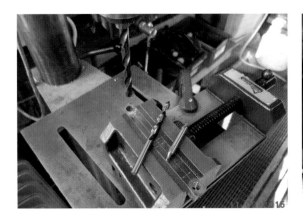

Drilling connecting rod for bearing.

Rough turn diameters.

Finish turn to shape.

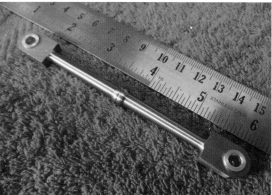

Finished connecting rod with bearings fitted.

Next, drill 8mm for the bearings. The exact size is not important as you will make the bearings to fit the hole, but it is important that you firmly clamp the vice to the drill table as this will help produce a nice clean hole. With one end of the bar supported with a running centre, and using the centre pops as a guide, rough out the shape of the con rod with a parting tool. Using a knife tool, rough out the rest of the con rod. Change over to a radius tool and with compound slide set at 1 ½ deg, generate the taper working towards the chuck. Swap the bar around and generate the taper on the other end to bring it to its final 'fish belly' shape. The ends are finished off using filing buttons.

Bearings Part G34

Turn the outside diameter for a tight push fit in the con rod, and assemble one 5mm bearing to one end and a 6mm bearing to the other for the crank shaft, using high strength Loctite.

Vertical Beam Assembly Part G18

Now I'm really going to push the fancy boat out! For my engine, I made this part to look like a series of interlocking rings. I first saw this type of cast iron work on a beam engine on display at Quarry Bank Mill, Styal, Cheshire and I've had a yearning to try

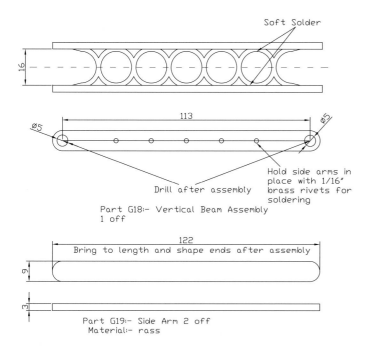

Soft Solder

16

113

Ø5   Ø5

Hold side arms in place with 1/16" brass rivets for soldering

Drill after assembly

Part G18:- Vertical Beam Assembly
1 off

122
Bring to length and shape ends after assembly

9

3

Part G19:- Side Arm 2 off
Material:- rass

Part G18 vertical beam assembly.

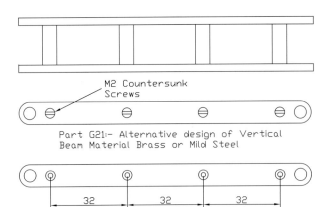

M2 Countersunk Screws

Part G21:- Alternative design of Vertical Beam Material Brass or Mild Steel

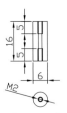

M2

Part G23:- Spacer for Alternative Beam 4 off Material:- Brass or Mild Steel

32   32   32

Part G22:- Alternative Side Arm

Part G21 alternative design of vertical beam.

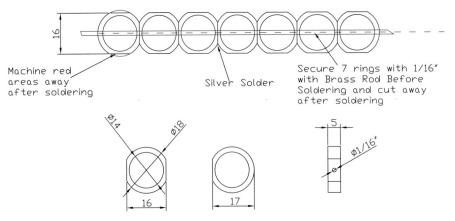

Machine red areas away after soldering

Silver Solder

Secure 7 rings with 1/16" with Brass Rod Before Soldering and cut away after soldering

Ø14   Ø18

16   17

5   Ø1/16"

Part G20:- Fabrication of interlocking rings Material:- Brass

Part G20 fabrication of interlocking rings.

modelling it ever since. But not to worry if you don't want to take on this challenge – you can build an alternative, but equally attractive, ladder rung design (part G22) that will be far simpler to make.

The interlocking rings are fabricated as shown in part G20. Start by turning the bar down to 18mm – a length long enough to make all seven rings plus an allowance for the width of the parting off tool. Put shallow grooves along the bar to designate each ring. Transfer the bar still in the chuck over to one of my favourite bits of kit – the spin indexer – and symmetrically mill two flats to give a width of 16mm. Then, down each side, drill a line of 1/16" holes. Return the chuck to the lathe drill 14mm and part the rings off to width.

Now comes the fun part! Pass a 1/16" brass rod through all of the rings to keep them orientated whilst you silver solder. To silver solder, give each joint a generous dollop of flux and on the top of each joint place a little nugget of silver solder. The parts are relatively light so you will get enough heat out of a plumber's hand-held burner with a propane/butane mix gas cartridge. Apply the heat indirectly at first: if you point the flame directly at the job all that will happen is that you will blow the nuggets off. Let it heat up slowly and when you see the flux start to melt and turn glassy, sticking the nuggets in place, direct the flame onto the job. When it comes up to temperature you will see the nuggets of solder melt. Slowly work along until all joints are mad. Allow to cool, and

Turning the rings.

Drilling rings out.

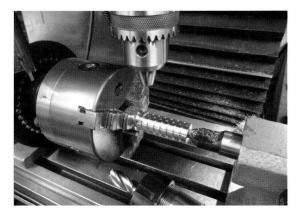

Drilling the rings using a spin indexer.

Parting rings off.

clean in a bath made up of citric acid. Remove from the bath, rinse with cold clean water, and tidy off any surplus solder with a file.

It will probably warp or go out of shape a little with the heat, so persuade it flat by squeezing it between the jaws of the vice. Then mount it in the mill and take equal amounts off each side to make it a width of 16mm.

Side Arms Part G19

These are fixed to the rings with soft solder. Being held in place for soldering with 1/16" brass rivets, the process is similar to the silver soldering except that you are using nuggets of soft solder, and you need far

Rings threaded together and set up for silver soldering.

Milling rings to width.

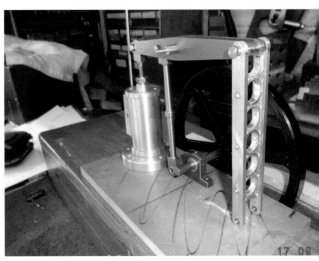

Trail assembly.

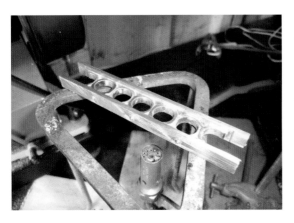

Soft soldering side arms.

less heat. Drill either end (5mm) and finally cut away the unwanted brass rod and half of the two end brass rings. Tidy everything up with a file and emery cloth.

Alternative Vertical Beam Part G21

The side Arms Part G22

Made from 3/8" x 1/8" mild steel, and using the same method as the horizontal beam engine so that they are drilled as a matching pair. The spacer part 23 is a simple turning job. Just try and get them all the same length and the whole lot is held together with M2 countersunk screws.

Swivel Base Part G24

This is a straightforward part so I won't say anything else about it.

Finished to final shape.

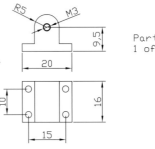

Part G24:- Swivel Base
1 off Material Mild Steel

Part G24 swivel base.

Eccentric Assembly Part G48

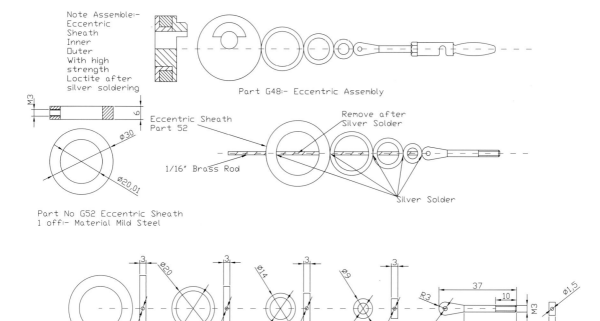

Note Assemble:-
Eccentric
Sheath
Inner
Outer
With high
strength
Loctite after
silver soldering

Part G48:- Eccentric Assembly

M3

Ø30

Ø20.01

Eccentric Sheath
Part 52

Remove after
Silver Solder

1/16" Brass Rod

Silver Solder

Part No G52 Eccentric Sheath
1 off:- Material Mild Steel

3   Ø20   3   Ø14   3   Ø9   3   37   10   Ø1.5

Ø1.5   Ø16   Ø10   Ø1.5   Ø5   Ø1.5   R3   Ø2   M3   25   3

Part G49:- Method of Fabrication 1 off Material Brass

Part G48 eccentric assembly, part G49 method of fabrication, part G52 eccentric sheath.

Eccentric Assembly: Part G49

Method of Fabrication: Part G52

Eccentric Sheath

This eccentric differs from the horizontal and the vertical engines in that it's a slip eccentric that allows the engine to be reversed. It's basically very similar but with a flat face that engages with a peg on the crank shaft. Apart from this the parts are very similar to the horizontal engine

Eccentric Sheath Assembly Part G49

I've pushed another boat out with this part in that I've continued the interlocking ring theme. It is manufactured in the same way as the vertical beam, except the rings reduce in size. The largest ring is the eccentric sheath and is connected to the eccentric valve link part G51.

Drawing part G50 shows an alternative simpler arrangement

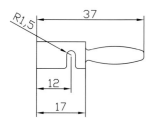

R1.5   37

12

17

6

M3

Part G51:- Eccentric
Valve Link 1 off
Material:- Mild Steel

Part G51 eccentric
valve link.

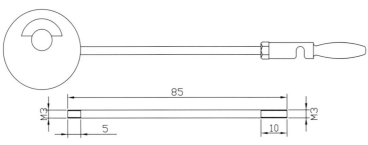

Part G50:- Alternative Eccentric Assembly

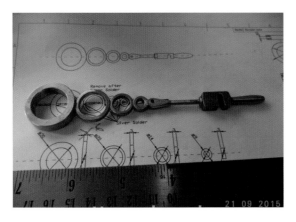

Eccentric arm complete assembly.

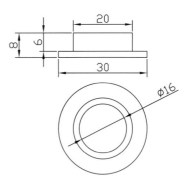

Part G53 Eccentric Inner 1 off
Material:- Mild Steel

Eccentric Outer G54

The eccentric outer is exactly the same as for the horizontal engine so requires no further explanation.

Eccentric Inner G53

Again, this is very similar to the horizontal engine except for the drive flat that has to be correctly oriented and accurately produced as this will affect the valve events. This is best done with the aid of a simple gauge (Sketch G1). It is made from a short stub of 5/16″ diameter bar taken off the same length of bar you will make the crank shaft from. To accurately drill through the centre line of the bar you will have to make yourself a drill bush. Again, using the same 5/16″ bar, centre drill and drill 3mm and part a small 4mm wide bush, then gripping the stub of bar in the drill vice and using the bush to guide the drill. Drill through 3mm – the hole will be perfectly on the centre line. Fix a short length of 3mm silver steel in the hole with super glue to make the gauge. Use this gauge to cut the flat in the correct orientation in the eccentric.

Part G54:- Eccentric Outer 1 off
Material:- Mild Steel

Part G53 eccentric inner part G54 eccentric outer.

The whole assembly is put together with high strength Loctite 603. Don't forget to put the eccentric sleeve in place, and to avoid contaminating the sleeve with adhesive which stops it rotating, put a few drops of the adhesive into the bore. That way, any surplus is pushed to the outside and out of harm's way.

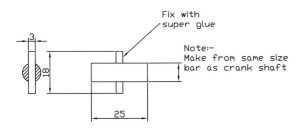

Sketch G1:- Eccentric sectioning gauge.

Eccentric drive flat gauge sketch G1.

Method of Fabrication Part G49

Turn up the four rings and drill the 1/16" cross hole in each ring and the M3 threaded end, thread them onto the 1/16" brass rod and silver solder them together as for the vertical beam.

Eccentric Valve Link Part G51

This is made from 3/8" square mild steel. Cut off a 40mm length and in the self-centring four-jaw drill and tap one end M3. Swap it round in the chuck and form a nice handle shape. Then, drill a 3mm cross hole, and cut and file it into a slot that's a nice slide fit on a piece of 3mm rod, and file down the width to 6mm.

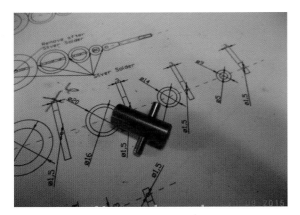

Eccentric drive flat gauge.

Form handle to shape.

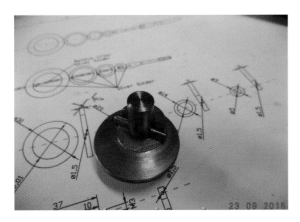

Eccentric with drive flat gauge.

If you do have a disaster, keep calm and don't panic. The adhesive bond is easily broken by applying a little heat. This is best done with one of those hot air paint striping guns.

Check fit.

Alternative Eccentric Assembly Part G50

This is a far simpler arrangement; the interlocking rings being replaced with a length of round bar.

Valve Linkage Assembly Part G55

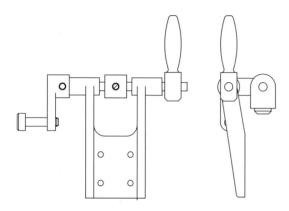

Part G55:- Valve Linkage Assembly

Part G55 valve linkage assembly.

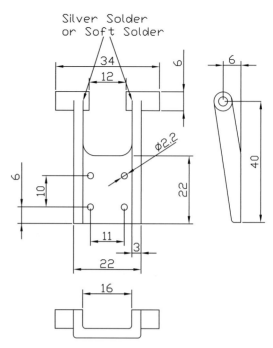

Silver Solder or Soft Solder

Part G60:- Valve Lever Bracket 1 off
Make from 1" Box section mild steel

Part G60 valve lever bracket.

Valve Lever Bracket Part G60

This is made from a piece of 1" square mild steel box section that will require silver soldering, or as the part is not stressed you could use soft solder. Cut off a 50mm length of box section and cut it down the middle length-wise, and file or mill the bottom face flat. Drill 6mm right through both sides to take the steel bush and drill the four 2.2mm bolting down holes. Turn up a bush 34mm long, 6mm outside diameter with a 3mm through hole. With a file, clean up the area around the 6mm hole back to bare metal so that the solder will stick, and solder the bush in place. Mill or file the lever to its final shape before cutting away the middle section of the steel bush.

Box section cut in half to make valve lever bracket.

Central Valve Crank Arm Part G57: Valve Crank Arm Part G58:

Both parts are made from 3/8" square mild steel bar: along a length of bar drill the 3mm holes 12.5mm apart and turn up a tight fitting 3mm mandrel-threaded M3. Clamp the arms one at a time to this mandrel, and in the lathe gently nibble the material away to form the 8mm diameter and finish off the radii with filling buttons. Don't forget to elongate the hole in the central valve crank arm, drill and tap M3 for grub screws.

Part filed square and flat.

Trail fit.

Drill bracket.

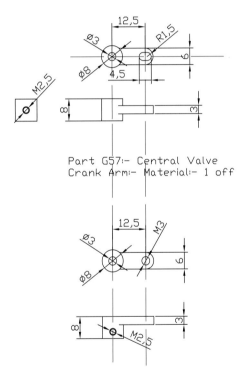

Part G57:- Central Valve
Crank Arm:- Material:- 1 off

Part G58:- Valve Crank Arm 1 off
Material Mild Steel

Part G59:- Valve crank Pin 1 Off
Material Mild Steel

Part G57 central valve crank arm, part G58 valve crank arm
part G59 valve crank pin.

Solder bush in bracket.

Turn arms to thickness on mandrel.

Trial assembly.

Valve Crank Pin Part G59

Made from mild steel which is just a simple turning with the thread cut with a die.

Forked Link Part G62

Made from 3/8" square mild steel bar in the four-jaw chuck face, centre drill and drill and tap M3. You'll find it easier to hold if you keep it on the bar to form the fork. First, drill the 3mm diameter cross hole then chain drill the slot for the fork. Then part it off from the bar and finish the slot off with files and file the radius using filing buttons. The link pin is just a 9mm length of 3mm silver steel fixed in the fork with a spot of superglue at assembly.

Swivel Pin Part G61

This is just a length of 3mm silver steel

Handles Part G56

These are made from ¼" square mild steel shaped in the lathe and drilled and tapped to take a M3 grub screw.

Cross Arm Assembly Part G40

It is important that the hole centres of both arms are the same, and the best way to do this is to use the same simple jig as used for the vertical engine

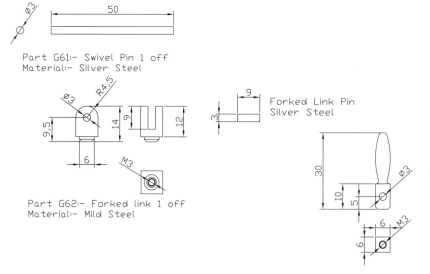

Part G61:- Swivel Pin 1 off
Material:- Silver Steel

Forked Link Pin
Silver Steel

Part G62:- Forked link 1 off
Material:- Mild Steel

Part G56:- Handle 1 off
Material 1/4" Squ Mils Steel

Part G56 handle part G62 forked link part G61 swivel pin.

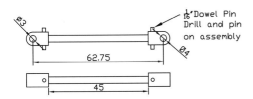

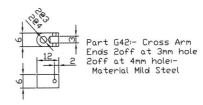

Part G42:- Cross Arm Ends 2off at 3mm hole 2off at 4mm hole:- Material Mild Steel

Part G40 Cross Arm Assembly 4 off:- Note 60mm hole centres to be drilled on jig sketch 1 same as vertical engine to maintain repeatability centres

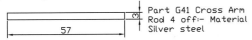

Part G41 Cross Arm Rod 4 off:- Material Silver steel

Part G40 cross arm assembly, part G41 cross arm rod, part G42 cross arm ends.

(Sketch V1). After assembling the parts together, drill one end of each arm and then, using the drilling jig firmly clamped on the drill table, drill the remaining hole. To check that they are the same simply pass two pieces of bar through both ends of the rod.

A Frame Assembly Part G26

It's important for the smooth action of the grasshopper motion that the frame is square to the beam to allow the two swinging cross arms to move freely. The best way to achieve this with modest kit is to give yourself some wriggle room by not making the fit of the parts too tight, so that you can make adjustment to the alignment. I've drawn up two alternative designs, one with interlocking rings and the other with plainer straight-sided sides. In terms of difficulty, I don't think there's much difference between the two.

A Frame Part G26 Or Alternative Part G27

To keep the theme the same, I made the interlocking ring design using ¼" x 1" thick mild steel bar

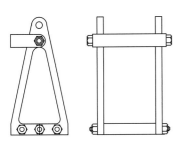

Part G26:- A Frame Assembly 1 Off

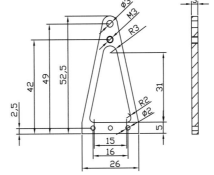

Part G27:- A Frame 2 Off Material:- Mild Steel

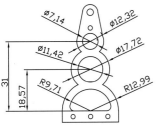

Part G28:- Alternative Geometry for A Frame.

Part G26 a frame assembly, part G27 a frame, alternative geometry for a frame.

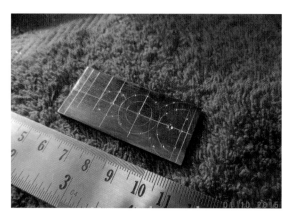

Marking out a frame.

Rough drill frame out.

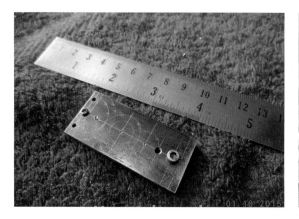

Frame parts fastened together to make a matching pair.

Saw and file to shape.

cut to length allowing a few mm extra on the length for squaring up and finishing. Square up using the mill or a file and set square, put a good dollop of marking blue or felt tip onto one face and mark out the hole position and the finished shape you want it to be. Mark the lines with light centre pops so that you don't lose them. Drill one hole right through both pieces and bolt the two parts together, then drill and tap the remaining functional holes. Drill out the decorative holes, and with a hack saw cut away the unwanted material and bring to the final shape using a range of different files. So you can assemble the parts in the same orientation as they were made and get a square assembly, mark the edge of each frame with a light centre pop mark.

The Base Part G29

Made from the same size bar as the frame, the first job is to square up the cut edges. Then, scribe a mark across the diagonals to find the centre and centre pop. Set the base up in the independent four-jaw chuck using the wobble bar method, centre drill, followed by a ½" drill then bore out to 16mm for a loose fit on the cylinder cover. Use the cover as a jig and, using the scribed diagonal lines as a guide, position the base squarely on the cover and clamp it. Spot through to mark the hole positions and drill through 3.2mm. Carefully mark out the position of M2 holes on one side only, and drill and tap them square. Screw one frame side piece in place and, in the same orientation as it was made with its partner, line up the other side piece and clamp it in place.

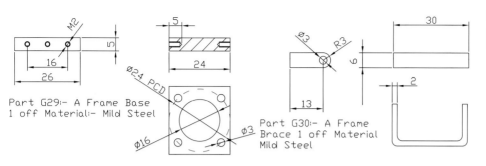

Part G29 base,
part G31 frame
brace.

Part G29:- A Frame Base
1 off Material:- Mild Steel

Part G30:- A Frame
Brace 1 off Material
Mild Steel

Bore out base.

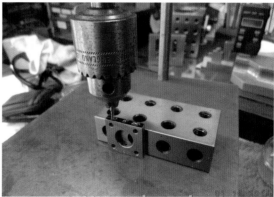

Tapping using tapping stand: – note use of square block.

Spot through as many of the holes as the clamp will allow you to get to. Drill and tap the holes, assemble the frame. Then drill and tap any remaining holes – with any luck you will end up with a reasonable square assembly.

Frame Brace Part G31

This is simply made from a length of mild steel cut from a piece of plate, drilled and bent to fit.

Crank Shaft Assembly Part G43

Normally, when you set the valve events on an engine, you tend to rotate the eccentric on the crank shaft, but with this slip eccentric design the position of the eccentric is fixed by the drive pin. Instead, you have to rotate the crank web so it is fixed to the crank shaft with an M3 grub screw. It's important that the eccentric drive pin is in the centre of the crank shaft. The easiest way to do this is to make yourself a drill bush from the same material that you make the shaft from.

The parts are straightforward enough to make and should pose no problems.

I'm not a great advocate for fixing the flywheel to the crank shafts of these small engines with keys or grub screws as these tend to induce a wobble in the flywheel which I find annoying. On the horizontal engine, I resorted to simply bolting the flywheel up against a shoulder turned on the end of the crank shaft. For the vertical engine I just used good old high strength Loctite. With this engine having a relatively thin flywheel, the contact area for the adhesive was insufficient to create a strong bond. I had to give it a little extra help by putting a straight knurl on the shaft to give it an extra bite in the flywheel which when combined with the Loctite secured the flywheel nice and concentric on the shaft.

Bedplate Part G85

This is made from a piece of ½" aluminium jig plate. Off cuts can be easily bought from the internet auction sites at a reasonable cost or, if you can't drop on

Part G43 crank shaft assembly, part G44 crank pin, part G45 crank web, part G46 crank shaft, part G47 eccentric drive pin.

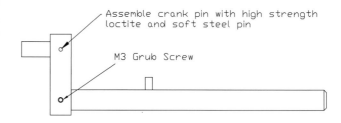

Assemble crank pin with high strength loctite and soft steel pin

M3 Grub Screw

Part G43:- Crank Shaft Assembly 1 off

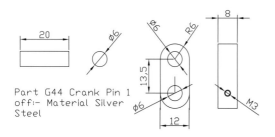

Part G44 Crank Pin 1 off:- Material Silver Steel

Part G45 Crank Web 1 off:- Material Mild Steel

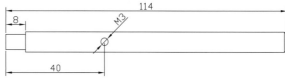

Part G46 Crank Shaft 1 off Material Mild Steel

Part G47:- Eccentric Drive Pin 1 off:- Material Silver Steel

Crank shaft given a straight knurl to retain flywheel.

a piece of aluminium of a suitable size, MDF will be perfectly acceptable. The cut outs for the crank can be easily chain drilled and filed out. Don't jump in with both feet by marking out all the holes and drilling and tapping them, or at least not without doing a trial assembly first. Drill and countersink the 4mm hole that will bolt the cylinder down first, then locate the bearing stand and the vertical beam and check them for position. With the horizontal beam set level,

mark where they go, and check against the drawing. If they are roughly correct go ahead and drill and tap.

You should have all the parts available to assemble the engine for a trial run, but for this you will need to make the wooden base (part G86) – more about this in a minute. I had a base left over from a previous engine build that I could use as a temporary test bed. Setting the valve events is somewhat more complicated by this engine's valve linkage and the angle of the eccentric rod to the axis of the crank shaft affecting the angle at which the eccentric is at top dead centre, compared with the crank. Whereas with the previous two engines the eccentric follows the crank by 90 degrees, with this engine it leads the crank by 45 degrees. It takes a little while to get your head round this at first, but once mastered setting the valves is quite straightforward. You first have to centralize the valve travel by observing its movement through the inlet port, making adjustments with the levers. Once you have the movement centralized and, when looking at the engine from the front, turn the flywheel clockwise ensuring that the drive pin is located on the eccentric flat. Position the eccentric in the fully forward position at the half past 10 position; the piston valve will be opening half the inlet port.

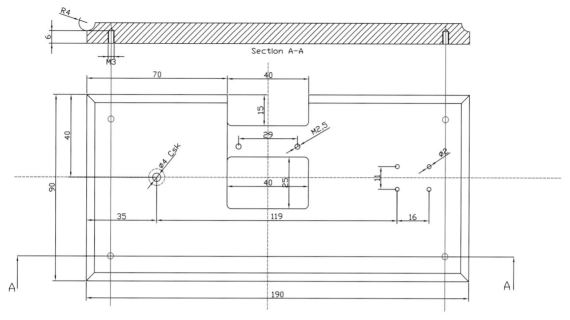

Section A-A

Part G85:- Bed Plate 1 off Material 1/2" Aluminium Jig Plate or MDF

Part G85 bed plate.

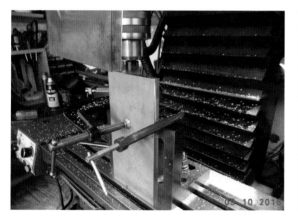

Squaring up bed plate in mill. Note use of angle plate and clamps.

Cutting out holes in bed plate using mill.

Slacken the crank grub screw and rotate it until it is at the 9 o'clock position and tighten the grub screw up good and tight to prevent the crank from slipping and messing the events up. Connect it up to the air and with a bit of luck it should run. If it doesn't and you are sure that you have the events set correctly, slowly go around the engine checking and dealing with any tight spots or areas that may be fouling. From experience I've found one of the best things to do is to slacken things off, and see if the engine runs. If it does, one by one tighten things up. If it stops, you've located a problem to deal with. To put the engine in reverse, disconnect the eccentric from the valve, reverse the flywheel until the drive pins locates on the other side of eccentric flat, re-connect the eccentric to the valve and it should now run the other way.

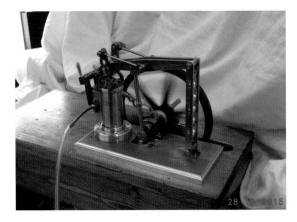

Trial run on test bed.

Finishing Off

Now is the time to add those little details that makes all the difference to the appearance of the engine. I wanted to make the base look like a stone-built engine house with a back wall to take a winding drum. Additionally, I added a regulator to give the engine driver a means of controlling the speed at which the wagons were hauled, and a whistle for the engine driver to sound to warn the men working on the bank that he was about to haul wagons so that they could get out of the way. Hi-visibility jackets weren't worn in those days. At this stage, it's up to you if you want to add these finishing touches: as the man said, 'It's your engine, lad, you can do anything you want to it.'

The Wooden Base Part G86

The base doesn't call for close fitting dovetail joints. It's glued and screwed together using those plastic chocolate block gizmos. It is made from rough chipboard with the stone courses cut and chiselled in, darkened with a black felt tip pen so that they stand out and stained with a brown water-based stain (which is sealed with a watered-down coat of PVA glue). The

Once I've got the engine running reasonably well, I like to give it a good run in with plenty of oil. To oil the cylinder, I simply squirt some oil down the plastic air pipe, connect the pipe up and let the air pressure take it into the cylinder. I've found that once the engine is run in and finally completed, it needs very little oiling. I've run engines for four or five hours without additional oiling.

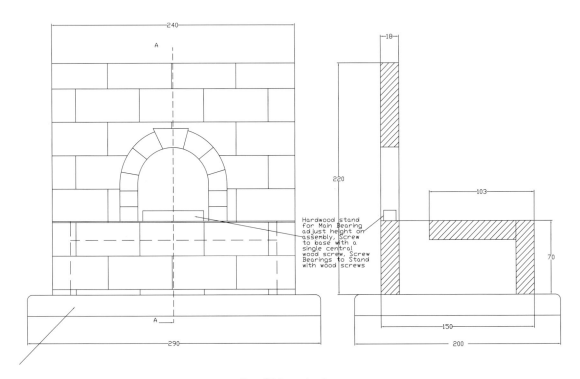

Part G86 wooden base.

Base glued and screwed.

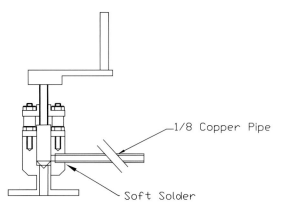

Part No G78:-
Regulator Assembly

Part G78 regulator assembly.

1/8 Copper Pipe

Soft Solder

rough chipboard gives a nice stone effect texture. The whole lot is screwed to a hard wood base just to neaten the effect up.

Regulator Assembly Part G78

This is more or less identical to the stop valve I used for the vertical engine, but the main difference is that I've replaced the hand wheel with a cranked handle that would have given the engine driver a finer control over the speed of the engine.

Whistle Assembly Part G68

The basic design for the whistle valve and whistle came from LBSC book *Shops, Shed and Road*, the bible for any builder of live steam models. It's mainly basic machining, but a couple of features do need a little more explanation.

Valve Body Part G70

This has a slot cut into it to take the lever. I machined this using a slitting saw in my mill, but don't panic – there is another way to achieve the same end. If you put two hacksaw blades in your hacksaw frame, with care you can cut a perfectly functional slot, and after a little attention with small files no one will know. Another little hacksawing tip: when cutting thin

sheets, use a blade with a higher tooth count for a smoother cut. The teeth won't straddle the material, jamb and break off.

Whistle Body Part G72

This is made from ¼" thin wall brass tube, and the mouth is easily filed to the general shape. When it comes to the disc part G73, LBSC was very specific about getting the correct shape of the cut out. This can be done by using your lathe as a shaper: first, you have to turn the disc up to a tight fit in the body, then using the part off tool and 2mm back from the front face machine an undercut. Switch the power off, turn the parting off tool on its side and set the top edge of the tool on centre. Set one of the chuck jaws to the vertical position, gently touch the tool onto the bar then put on a 0.05 cut and wind the tool across the face until it passes into the undercut. Take it back to the start. Rotate the chuck slightly and take the tool across again another slight rotation until the jaw is at 4 o'clock position. Set it back vertical, put another cut on and repeat until you've gone to the desired depth. To square up the other corner, set the tool bottom edge on centre, and square it out as before. When you are happy that you have the desired shape, part the disc off. The rest of the parts are straightforward enough to make. The body, disc and connector part G74 can be assembled with soft solder or superglue.

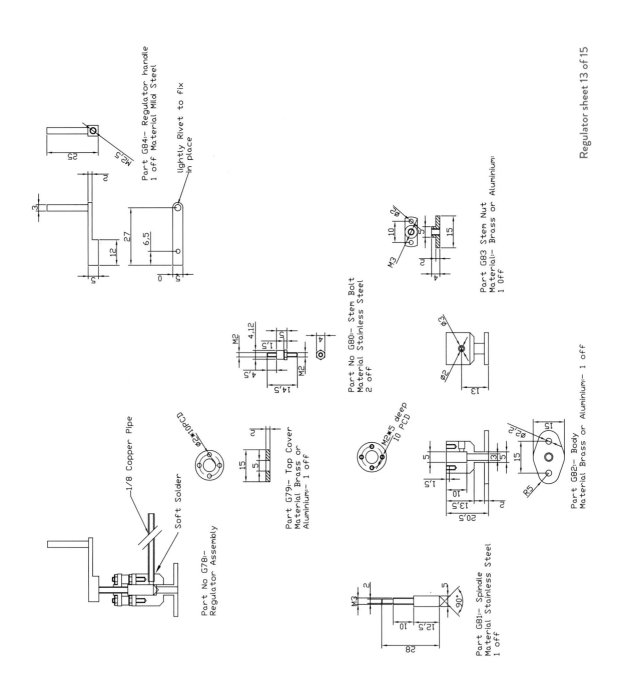

Part G84:- Regulator handle
1 off Material Mild Steel

lightly Rivet to fix
in place

Part No G78:-
Regulator Assembly

1/8 Copper Pipe

Soft Solder

Part G79:- Top Cover
Material Brass or
Aluminium:- 1 off

Part No G80:- Stem Bolt
Material Stainless Steel
2 off

Part G81:- Spindle
Material Stainless Steel
1 off

Part G82:- Body
Material Brass or Aluminium:- 1 off

M2*5 deep
10 PCD

Part G83 Stem Nut
Material:- Brass or Aluminium:-
1 off

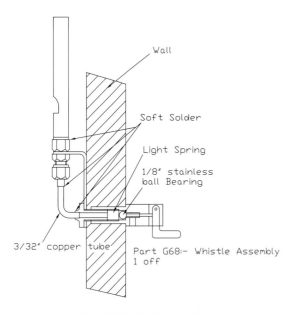

Part G68 whistle assembly.

24TPI hacksaw blade.

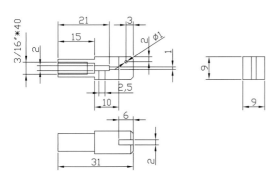

Part G70:- Valve Body 1 off
Material:- Brass

Part G70 valve body.

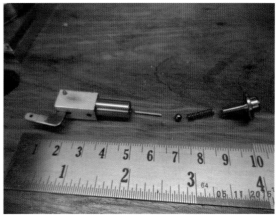

Whistle valve parts.

The remaining parts, numbers G69, G75, G71, G76, G77, are all straightforward and should pose little problem. The commercially supplied 3/16" X 40 ME union nut is readily available from any of the suppliers to the hobbyist.

Using slitting saw on whistle body.

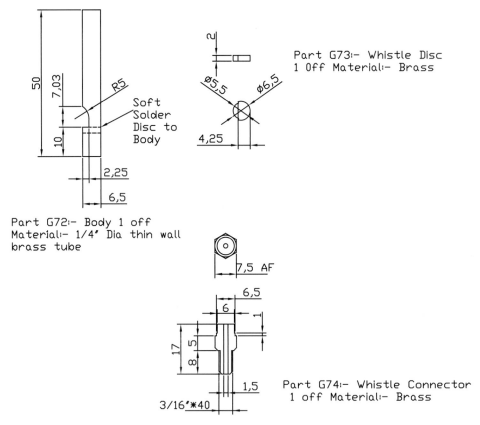

Part G73:- Whistle Disc
1 Off Material:- Brass

Part G72:- Body 1 off
Material:- 1/4" Dia thin wall
brass tube

Soft
Solder
Disc to
Body

7,5 AF

Part G74:- Whistle Connector
1 off Material:- Brass

Part G72 body, part G73 whistle disc, part G74 whistle connector.

Mouth of whistle shaped.

Using lathe to shape disc to required shape.

Correct disc shape. Note sharp corners.

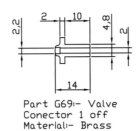

Part G69:- Valve
Conector 1 off
Material:- Brass

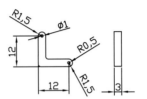

Part G69:- Valve
Conector 1 off
Material:- Brass

Part G71:- Lever 1 off
Material:- Mild Steel

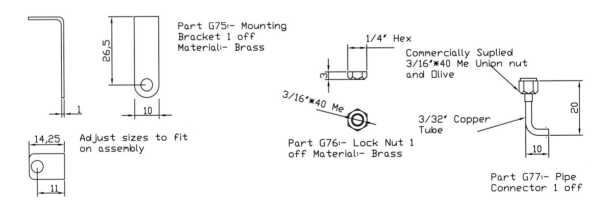

Part G75:- Mounting
Bracket 1 off
Material:- Brass

1/4" Hex

Commercially Suplied
3/16"*40 Me Union nut
and Olive

3/16"*40 Me

3/32' Copper
Tube

Adjust sizes to fit
on assembly

Part G76:- Lock Nut 1
off Material:- Brass

Part G77:- Pipe
Connector 1 off

Part G69 valve connector: part G75 mounting bracket: part G71 lever: part G76 locknut: part G77 pipe connector.

All that's now required is to remove all the sharp edges from the parts that are to be painted, thoroughly de-grease them, give the non-ferrous parts a flash of acid etch primer, prime the ferrous parts with a suitable ferrous primer, carefully reassemble the parts sealing the joints with a suitable sealer, set the valve events and sit back and admire your work.

Valve and whistle parts.

The three completed engines. Left to right: Cross Single, Grasshopper and Horizontal.

8 Your Next Challenge Is?

WELL, THAT'S THE TRIO of engines completed. I hope you have enjoyed following my builds in this book as much as I enjoyed designing and building them. You don't tend to stand still in this game. I'm currently building a locomotive – a 5" Gauge 2-6-0 Horwich Crab. In the meantime, I hope some of you have been inspired by this book to have a go at designing your own engine, using the methods and procedures based around the standard kit of parts. So just to get you going here are a few suggestions:

- Beam engine using Watts parallel motion
- Vertical marine-type engine with Stevens reversing gear
- Self-contained horizontal engine (this type had the cylinders bolted onto the end of the bedplate with the other end opening out to contain the crank shaft bearings)
- Table engine with the cross head above the cylinder and long cranks operating underneath
- V twin with cylinders at 90 degrees to each other acting on a single crank shaft

There are plenty of examples out there for you to draw inspiration from. Don't get too hung up about making a perfect scale model. The important thing is for you to work safely and to enjoy the process.

Acknowledgements

I WOULD LIKE TO thank the online community of worldwide model engineers without whose stimulation, help and guidance this book couldn't have been produced. I would also like to thank the members of the South Cheshire Model Engineering Society for their friendship, and in particular Peter Cauley and John Hughes for unstinting advice and wise guidance.

I was fortunate to be born into a large family of aunts, uncles and cousins who, along with my parents, lavished love and attention on me during my formative years, and instilled in me the virtue of honest hard work.

Finally, I would like to thank my own close family: my son Alistair and daughter Kirstin, and their partners Katherine and Paul, and my fantastic grandchildren Joshua, Eleanor, Matthew and Duncan who have all patiently indulged me in my model engineering activities.

A special thank you to my wife Dorothy, 'the boss', whose love and support has helped and influenced me in many of my life's achievements and suffers with great patience long rambling discussions about my latest model engineering project.

Appendix: Stationary Steam Engines on Exhibition

OR THOSE OF YOU who wish to seek out examples of stationary engines on display, there are many well-preserved examples in the United Kingdom that have been beautifully restored and maintained in working order by various societies and are manned by a dedicated volunteer workforce of enthusiast. The list comprises only examples that I'm aware of. I'm often amazed at some of the unusual places I come across examples of stationary engines, for example stately homes under the guardianship of the National Trust and I've even come across examples on a city's roundabout proudly advertising its industrial past. Whenever I come across an example, I can't resist taking photographs to file away for use in a future project.

Northern Mill Engine Society

The society was formed in 1966 and is based in what was the cotton store of a spinning mill. It is home to one of the largest collection of stationary engines in the UK, many of them running on steam. The society regularly holds steaming days for the public:

Bolton Steam Museum, Mornington Road, Off Chorley Old Road, Bolton BL14EU
Phone 01204 846490 or 01257 265003
https://www.nmes.org/index.html

Quarry Bank Mill Styal Cheshire

Run by the National Trust, the mill was established by Samuel Gregg in 1874. It is situated on the banks of the River Boland that provided the water power for the mill. The mill wheel is still operational. The mill itself is now powered by electricity via line shafting but still retains the textile machinery that is demonstrated daily. There is a steam-driven beam engine and a horizontal engine, as well as a number of smaller engines and machinery on display:

Quarry Bank Mill, Styal, Wilmslow, Cheshire, SK9 4HP
Email: quarrybank@nationaltrust.org.uk
Phone 01625 527468
https://www.nationaltrust.org.uk/quarry-bank

Science and Industry Museum

The museum is dedicated to Manchester's rich history of innovation and scientific discoveries that changed the world during the industrial revolution. It has many exhibits and displays showing the machinery that drove this huge period of change, including many stationary steam engines many of which are still in working order.

Science and Industry Museum, Liverpool Road, Manchester, M3 4FP
Email: info@ScienceMuseumGroup.ac.uk
Email: info@sciencemuseumgroup.ac.uk
Phone 033 0058 0058
https://www.scienceandindustrymuseum.org.uk/visit

Science Museum

The Science Museum is the capital's pre-eminent museum, dedicated to extraordinary human achievements and technological advances. Through the year it holds special events and exhibition covering all aspect of science and industry, and has a number of stationary engines in its exhibition:

Exhibition Road, South Kensington, London, SW7 2DD
Phone 033 0058 0058
https://www.sciencemuseum.org.uk/

Levant Mine and Beam Engine

Perched on the cliffs overlooking the sea, you couldn't get a more dramatic setting for a stationary steam engine. The mine was started in 1820 and finally closed 1930, and was passed into the care of the National Trust in 1967. The mines whim engine (winding engine) was restored by a group of volunteers known as the 'Greasy Gang', and today the engine can be seen in action as the last of its kind to work under steam in its original engine house:

Trewellard, Pendeen, near St Just, Cornwall, TR18 7SX
Phone: 01736 786156
Email: levant@nationaltrust.org.uk
https://www.nationaltrust.org.uk/levant-mine-and-beam-engine

Stott Park Bobbin Mill

Nestling on the shore of Lake Windermere in Cumbria, this steam-driven mill produced millions of wooden bobbins for the Lancashire spinning and weaving industry in its time. Now in the care of English Heritage, it is the only working bobbin mill left in the Lake District.

Finsthwaite, Ulverston, Cumbria, LA12 8AX
Phone 01539 531087
https://www.english-heritage.org.uk/visit/places/stott-park-bobbin-mill/

Crofton Beam Engines

The Crofton Pumping Station was built in 1808 to supply water to the highest point of the Kennet and Avon Canal which links London to Bristol. Rebuilt and modernized several times during its long working life, it had one of the two original Bolton and Watt steam powered engines running until 1958. The Kennet and Avon Trust bought the pumping station for preservation in 1968, and by 1971 both engines had been restored to working order:

Crofton Beam Engines, Crofton Pumping Station, Crofton, Marlborough, SN8 3DW
Phone 01672 870300
Email: crofton@katrust.org.uk
https://www.croftonbeamengines.org/

Beamish

Beamish is a living working museum that uses its collection to connect with people and tell the story of everyday life in the Northeast of England. The winding engine in the colliery exhibition, housed in a stone-built engine house, is the sole survivor of a type common to the northern coal fields:

Beamish Museum, Regional Resource Centre, Beamish, County Durham, DH9 0RG
Phone: 0191 3794000
Email: museum@beamish.org.uk
https://www.beamish.org.uk/

Papplewick Pumping Station

Scheduled as an Ancient Monument under the control of the Papplewick Pumping Station Trust, this is a registered charity dedicated to the preservation of the pumping station. The trust holds regular steaming days throughout the year. Built in the 1880s to pump millions of gallons of clean water to the city of Nottingham, the builders excelled themselves in the beauty and architectural details of the station's building:

Papplewick Pumping Station, Rigg Lane, Ravenshead,
Phone 0115 9632938
Email: director@papplewickpumpingstation.org.uk
http://www.papplewickpumpingstation.org.uk/

Mill Meece Pumping Station

Built by the Staffordshire and Potteries Water Board in the early 1900s, to supply water pumped from artesian to the potteries and Staffordshire. The engines are of the horizontal compound type, and the society holds regular steaming days throughout the year together with a range of themed rallies of historical interest:

The Mill Meece Pumping Station Preservation Trust, Coats Heath, Near Eccleshall, Staffordshire, ST21 6QU
Phone 01785 822138
Email: info@millmeecepumpingstation.co.uk
http://www.millmeecepumpingstation.co.uk/

Suppliers to the Model Engineering Hobbyist

HERE IN THE **U**NITED **K**INGDOM, we are blessed by a wide range of suppliers to the hobbyist many of whom will ship around the world. But I know that there are many model engineering enthusiasts in Europe, North America and Australia so I'm sure there will also be suppliers to the hobbyist there. The following list is of the main suppliers in the UK that I'm aware of and that I have used from time to time, but I hasten to add that I have no commercial arrangements with these companies. I have also used one of the internet trading and action sites – these are useful for picking up the odd item or material that is unobtainable from one of the main suppliers. But you have to be careful when buying off the internet that you are getting what you want: I once bought a 1000 M2 nuts for under £5. When I received them I found that 10 to 20 per cent of them had not been threaded; clearly someone was getting rid of defective stock. I still thought I got a bargain though!

Blackgates Engineering

Blackgates is a long-established supplier to the hobbyist. They stock a good range of material and tooling, and specialize in the supply of drawings and casting for model locomotives and traction engines, tooling fasteners and stationary engines:

Unit 1 Victory Court, Flagship Square, Shaw Cross Business Park, Dewsbury, West Yorkshire, WF12 7TH
Phone 01924 466000
Email: sales@blackgates.co.uk
http://www.blackgates.co.uk/

Reeves 2000

Reeves is another long-established supplier. They stock a good range of material and tooling, and specialize in the supply of drawings and casting for model locomotives, traction engines, tooling, fasteners and stationary engines:

Reeves 2000, Appleby Hill, Austry, Warwickshire, CV9 3ER
Phone 01827 830894
Email: sales@ajreeves.com
https://www.ajreeves.com/

Polly Model Engineering Limited incorporating Bruce Engineering

Polly Model specializes in the supply of locomotive self-build kits along with stationary engine kits, material, fasteners and tooling:

Polly Model Engineering Ltd, Atlas Mills, Birchwood Avenue, Long Eaton, Nottingham, NG10 3ND
Phone 0115 9736700
Email: sales@pollymodelengineering.co.uk
https://pollymodelengineering.co.uk/

Stuart Models

Stuart Models is an old, established firm. It is the oldest company in the world committed to supplying a wide range of model steam engines that can be supplied as a pre-machined kit or as a set of castings:

Stuart Models, Grove Works, West Road, Bridport, Dorset, DT6 5JT
Phone 01308 456869
https://www.stuartmodels.com/

Macc Models

Macc Models specialize in the supply of bar stock material as well as having an extensive range of tooling and steam fitting:

Macc Models, 45a Saville Street, Macclesfield, SK11 7LQ
Phone 0161 408 2938
Email: hello@maccmodels.co.uk
https://maccmodels.co.uk/

RDG Tools

RDG Tools stocks an extensive range of tools including a wide range of new and used machine tools and supplies to industry as well as the model engineering community:

RDG Tools Ltd, White Lee, Burnley Road, Mytholmroyd, West Yorkshire, HX7 5AD
Phone 01422 885069
Email: rdgtools@aol.com
https://www.rdgtools.co.uk/index.html

Arc Eurotrade

Supplier of a wide range of machine tools specifically for model engineering, along with an extensive range of tooling:

Arc Euro Trade, 10 Archdale Street, Syston, Leicester, LE7 1NA
Phone 0116 2695603
https://www.arceurotrade.co.uk

Tracy Tools

Another long-established family run firm that specializes in the supply of cutting tools, in both metric and imperial sizes:

Tracy Tools Ltd, Unit 1, Parkfield Units, Barton Hill Way, Torquay, TQ2 8JG
Phone 01803 328603
Email: info@tracytools.com
https://www.tracytools.com/

Noggin Ends

Supplier of small quantities of raw material specifically for the hobbyist including aluminium, brass, bronze, cast iron, steel, copper and copper alloys, engineering plastics, etc:

Noggin End Metals, Ashdown, 10 Boon Hill Road, Bignall End, Stoke on Trent, ST7 8LA
Phone 01782 865428
Email: mike@nogginend.com
https://www.nogginend.com/

Laser Master

This is the company who cut the flywheel for my grasshopper engine they had the drawing for my flywheel and I know that others have ordered from them.

Laser Master, Unit 23, United Downs Ind Park, Redruth, Cornwall, TR16 5HY
Phone 01209 821902
Email: sales@lasermaster.co.uk
https://www.lasermaster.co.uk/

Index

ISBN 978 1 78500 765 1

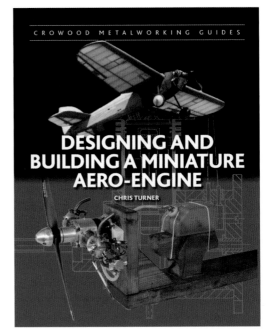

ISBN 978 1 84797 776 2

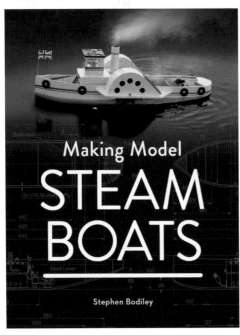

ISBN 978 0 71984 131 6

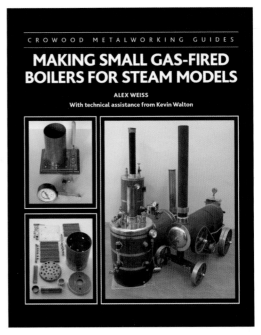

ISBN 978 1 78500 876 4